Chair

D1331346

Chair

Anne Massey

REAKTION BOOKS

Published by Reaktion Books Ltd
33 Great Sutton Street
London EC1V 0DX, UK

www.reaktionbooks.co.uk

First published 2011

Printed and bound in China by C&C Offset Printing Co., Ltd

British Library Cataloguing in Publication Data
Massey, Anne.
  Chair. — (Objekt)
  1. Chair design. 2. Chair design — History. 3. Chair
  design — Social aspects.
  I. Title II. Series
  749.3'2–dc22

ISBN 978 1 86189 758 9

Contents

Introduction

The chair is such a common, everyday object in the modern world. In the West we take it for granted that we can sit to eat in the public space of a café or restaurant, sit to work at the computer or to relax in the domestic setting of home. So the chair is a ubiquitous object, used extensively for our individual comfort, for staking out territory, for displaying power, for signifying the designer's presence or the craftworker's skills. But it is the chair's taken-for-grantedness that makes it such a fascinating object to deconstruct and account for. Like any cultural construction, this unassuming piece of furniture has a complex history and set of meanings. No other object characterizes the impact of modernity with such clarity. No other object offers the designer such an infinite range of possibilities to create an object that will be so intimately close to a stranger's body. This book sets out to scratch beneath the surface of the chair, to find out what lies beyond the textile upholstery or the plastic seat, the leather-covered squab or the woven cane support.

Anatomically, our bodies are not particularly suited to sitting on a chair; sitting on the ground is a better option for our health and for our backs. And a sizeable proportion of the world's population sits on the ground to eat, work and relax.[1] Our happiest times are probably spent not sitting on a chair – at a picnic, on the beach, playing on the

Herman Miller 2005 publicity shot, 'Impress the Neighbours', for a 20th-century design classic, the Eames lounge chair and ottoman.

floor with children, lying on the sofa watching television, or in bed with a lover. This may seem like celebration of a pre-industrial idyll, but scientific evidence points to the damage chairs do to our bodies. But the chair is a vital ordering device in modern, Western culture. It is a structure that holds our body above the ground in a seated position. The chair marks out our place in the modern world. It is a bridge between our body and the surrounding space. The chair acts as crucial cue for performativity. We interact with others in predetermined ways when seated; the chair can guarantee physical proximity or physical distance. Even in cultures that do not privilege the chair, a slow move towards its use is in evidence, stimulated by modernity and globalization. The Western chair has been slowly adopted in Asia and Africa, usually as signifiers of ultimate power and modernity.

Before modernity made such an impact in the East, or even in the West, there were very few chairs in existence or in use. The chair was a ceremonial device, used to signify the head of state or church, the lord of the manor or the bishop in his cathedral. Most of the

Girls sitting and enjoying a picnic, early 20th century.

population sat in subservience on benches or the floor. From the eighteenth century onwards, an explosion in consumer culture meant a greater proliferation of chair production and distribution; it became emblematic of the head of the household, rather than the head of state or church. By the Victorian era, all members of the affluent household had access to a chair, from the upholstered needlework chair for the women of the house, to the Windsor chair in the kitchen for the servants. The power of the chair as signifier in recent times has infiltrated the contemporary media, from the Eames chair in *Frasier* to the dreaded *Mastermind* chair on BBC television and the chair in the diary room of *Big Brother*. The chair marks important stages in our lives, not as all-pervasive as the cradle to the grave, but from the high chair to the bath chair is fairly inclusive. This is interjected by the school chair, the high stool in the teenagers' coffee bar, the formality of the dining chair, the comfort of the three-piece suite, with hopefully not too many sessions in the dentist's chair. Apart from marking stages in our lives, the power of the chair to represent core relationships in particular places remains as strong as ever. The Chair of a meeting sits at the table head; the power relations within homes are marked by chairs. It acts as a crucial signifier of power, and this was the chair's primary and earliest function. Spaces are marked out by the hierarchy of chairs, our place within the lecture room, the church, the restaurant or the pub is indicated by the chair we sit on, or aspire to sit on, and can't. The chair is such a personal, anthropomorphic object. Personal, individual, the chair can communicate the authority of the owner, the sitter, the designer. The directness of touch, the presence of a human body, an aura we can sense, left by the previous sitter.

The chair has a strong anthropomorphic aspect to its structure, with legs, arms, back and seat. So it can represent its designer, or its owner, in their absence. And this is a central feature of the modernist designer's relationship with the chair as cultural object. The materiality of the chair can communicate a culture's relationship with nature and issues of sustainability. Also, our bodies have an intimate relationship with the chairs we sit on, the coldness of black leather, the warm comfort of velvet, the familiarity of wood next to our skin. Contemporary designers, artists and architects play with the materiality of the chair form, and juxtapose surprising contrasts of materials – wicker and plastic; acid-coloured prints and sleek, black plastic; corrugated cardboard and hardboard. The chair can become a piece of artwork in itself, for example in the work of pop artist Allen Jones and Droog designer Jurgen Bey.

The chair in the modern period has largely been accounted for as a special, collector's object, in isolation, almost like a piece of sculpture. It is an object seen in a vacuum, an object for intense contemplation or veneration. Furniture history tends to consider the chair from the point of view of the designer or maker. The user or owner is sporadically included, but the patron is frequently aristocratic and wealthy. Where the life history of the object is considered, it is often the more exclusive and expensive chair that has been preserved, and its provenance and influence fetishized. There are also many histories of the chair that concentrate on the technical developments of its construction, for example the innovative use of bentwood. However, this then neglects the role of the end user and the impact of mass production. There are examples of leading design historians creating accounts of the creation and use of popular furniture in the West, in particular Penny Sparke's *Furniture* (1986). Judy Attfield's book, *Wild Things: The Material Culture of Everyday Life* (2000), included an analysis of the chair in the first chapter, 'Chairs Don't Grow on Trees: Defining Design'. Both works include the chair as part of a more general investigation of a bigger subject, and work as an important starting point for this book, which is the first to

consider the cultural history and meaning of the chair. To understand the subject more fully, we need to consider the chair within its broader context. Whether it is on a museum plinth, an advertisement, a suburban lounge, a Viennese coffee house, Victorian schoolroom or in our homes, the chair is an object that resonates and connects with its surrounding space. It also connects with the sitter, not just in terms of physical posture, but in terms of clothing and shoes – the restrictive corsets of the nineteenth century prohibited women from lounging, while barefooted beatniks could curl up on a chair with a book.

The first chapter considers the history of the chair in relation to power relations, from Egyptian times to the mid-twentieth century, using the prism of the end-user and spectator to provide a map for reading this complex history. I then turn to look at the very special relationship between the modern designer and the chair, and consider

Photo of Union Castle Line staff, c. 1960, Cape Town, South Africa.

the perennial problem of the authentic and the copy. By contrast, I then look at the interior decorator and the chair, using the theme of luxury and comfort. How designer/makers have worked with the form of the chair is then considered as a different strand, with an emphasis on surprising materials and unusual techniques. The book concludes by turning its attention to modern artists, and how they have recently played with the chair.

So the book plots the biography of an object, the chair. The subject of the chair for a book seemed relatively straightforward to begin with. Chairs are everywhere, and everybody uses them. There is a lot written about chairs. There is the antique collector's viewpoint, the well-trodden history of the designer chair in high modernism, and recent accounts of the one-off – craft or is it fine art? – object. However, it was the power relations determined by the Western use of this object for sitting that especially caught my attention. And I learned that not everyone can sit in a chair. At the early stages of working on the book, my new partner was diagnosed with cancer. We were 100 per cent hopeful he would make a full recovery; there is little else you can believe. And so began a relentless eighteen months of hospital and clinic appointments, treatments and operations. And it was the patterns of use, the distribution of power in the medical environments we visited, that prompted me to think about chairs differently, as instrumental in reinforcing social hierarchies. Doctors would make sure you were sitting down to receive bad news, whilst they frequently stood. The patient lies or sits whilst the nurse stands to attend. This eventually presented an insurmountable problem, since trying to find a comfortable chair for my partner when the cancer spread to his bones was an impossible task. His inability to sit in a chair reinforced his invalidity as a person, unable to join in accepted social interactions or be a good patient. He couldn't simply *Take a seat.*

I spent many hours sitting in an uncomfortable armchair in a hospice, watching him sadly deteriorate on the bed, with nurses and doctors darting in and out, standing around the bed, dispensing medicine, looking at each other, at their notes, at me and at him. In modern, Western culture we are poorly equipped to deal with death. It is hidden away, not spoken of. At the funeral friends and family sat on hard, pale, wooden benches provided by the crematorium, together in grief, in the same position, equal. But once at the wake, territories were staked with the pub chairs; intimate groups formed; old bonds were renewed. We were back to the reassuring normality of clusters of humanity, resting on wood and leatherette, metal and *moquette*, separated by our chair backs, brought together by the arrangement of our seats, reassured that it wasn't our turn just yet. We hopefully had many years of sitting in many chairs to come.

The historian Leora Auslander beautifully outlined the personal power of the chair in the introduction to her book *Taste and Power: Furnishing Modern France*:

> I have been made by that chair and I have made the chair. The chair was full of meanings over which I had no control, and of which I had only partial knowledge when I acquired it. In my home it acquired new meanings. My guests have a certain understanding of me when they arrive in my home; as a result of viewing my chair they have somewhat different understandings. In their eyes I become different – perhaps also in my own.[2]

In this book, whether it is in terms of the designers, the sitters or myself whilst writing, I relate the chair to the personal, to the lived experience. The emotional and sensual sides of life experience cannot be avoided. A contemporary advertisement by the Spanish furniture makers Stua featured their modernist Nube armchair:

The design of the Nube armchair comes from the combination between the flat orthodoxy of the contemporary spaces with the curves of the human body. While the outside lines of the Nube armchair are made of flat parallel surfaces, the space where we can sit is curved and cosy, like a nest.[3]

So let's now explore the history and development of this ubiquitous cultural object.

A back-street chair repair shop, southern France, 2007.

1 Seats of Power

I have power, because I am a Chair, in the sense that I am a university professor. This relationship between the chair and authority dates back to the fifteenth century, when meetings were first chaired, and it continues today.[1] This humble object can also mark out space and define territory, excluding the rest of the world and creating a powerful presence at the same time:

> Desperate for the waiters to leave, he [Edward] and Florence turned in their chairs to consider the view of a broad mossy lawn, and beyond, a tangle of flowering shrubs and trees clinging to a steep bank that descended to a lane that led to the beach.[2]

When did the power of the chair to include and exclude, to display power, to signal intimacy – as in this case – begin? It dates back some 4,000 years to the time of the ancient Egyptians, when the chair first became a vital signifier of power relations and social mores. At that time the chair reflected the status of the individual who commissioned and used it. And up until the nineteenth century the vast majority of the world's population had experience only of looking at a dignitary sitting in a chair, as opposed to sitting on one themselves. Whether pharaoh, maharaja, pope or emperor, the chair was reserved largely for the elite. With the impact of modernity, new economic, political and social forces meant that the chair became more common in everyday life, and was used to display hierarchies of power; different chairs were used by different sections of society, within both the Victorian domestic and public spheres in the West. Forms of Western etiquette and culture have been gradually assimilated globally, with the infiltration of modernity. The relationship between socio-political power and the chair changed dramatically, from being a signifier of the elite during the time that they were scarce, to a tool for suppression as they became ubiquitous in the nineteenth and twentieth centuries. This chapter charts the process.

The origin of the word chair itself lies in representations of power. Originating from the Greek noun *kathedra*, deriving from *kata* 'down' and *hedra* 'seat', *kathedra* meant an important chair, one used by a teacher or professor. This was adopted into Latin as *cathedra*. In late Latin this transformed into *cathedralis*, to mean 'belonging to the bishop's seat'. The word cathedral was then used in English from the thirteenth century as an adjective to denote a bishop's church in the sense of a *cathedral church*, the place where the bishop's seat could be found. This was shortened simply to *cathedral* by the sixteenth century. The word chair derives from this Greek origin. Whilst the bishop sat in a ceremonial chair, and the priests in stalls on either side, the congregation knelt on stone floors, reinforcing power relations. The use of the term Chair to denote a professor also stems from this etymology.

The earliest examples of chairs date back to ancient Egypt and the time of the Old Kingdom and the Fourth Dynasty (2613–2498 BC), when the vast majority did not experience the status of owning or even sitting on a chair. This was reserved for the upper echelons of society. The chair in ancient Egypt was a device to distinguish the elite by raising them physically to a higher level than that of

the peasants and slaves, who squatted on the ground – the hierarchy of society was set out by means of the chair. This is particularly visible in Egyptian statues, which reinforced the status of the sitters by means of chairs or thrones. The high point of ancient Egyptian culture was the New Kingdom, where the location of central power was Thebes (today's Luxor) from 1550 to 1069 BC. The monumental temples there and at Karnak were built and expanded by a succession of powerful pharaohs, supported by a vast army of priests, administrators and craftworkers. The pair of immense Eighteenth Dynasty (c. 1550–1295 BC) limestone statues represents the power of Amenhotep III. Reaching an impressive 18m (59ft) into the sky, the enthroned figures were erected to protect his mortuary temple on the west bank of the Nile. The culture of building pyramids had been superseded by

Egyptian limestone statue of Amenhotep III, 18th Dynasty. Luxor, Egypt.

underground tombs, carved into the limestone of the arid Valley of the Kings. This was to evade the thieves who regularly raided the tombs, since they were filled with treasures and rare objects, placed in the tombs with the mummified body of the pharaoh for the afterlife.

Since the tombs were deliberately secreted in the hillside, there is a constant process of discovery and 62 have been located to date. Because of the culture of packing the tombs with objects for the afterlife and the dry and hot weather conditions of Egypt, many

Tutankhamun's Throne, Egyptian Museum, Cairo, Egypt, 18th Dynasty.

chairs have survived the 3,000 years since their original incarceration. The most famous tomb is that of Tutankhamun (1336–1327 BC). Discovered by Howard Carter in 1922, the tomb contained a vast array of treasures, including ritual objects, weaponry, games, jewellery and furniture. The antechamber and annexe of the tomb were packed with a selection of stools and chairs, stacked haphazardly. Six chairs were found in the tomb in total, the most famous one being the Golden Throne. Now on display in the Cairo Museum, the regal chair was originally wrapped in black linen and was found in the antechamber, wedged beneath the Ammut couch.

The throne is made of wood and decorated with gold and silver sheets ornamented with semi-precious stones and glass. The sloping back is the main focus of the chair, and it is decorated with an image of the seated Tutankhamun and his queen, Ankhesenamun. The other five chairs discovered in the tomb include a finely carved, African ebony chair with ivory inlay and gold-leaf decoration and an important example of a backed folding stool, known as the Ecclesiastical Throne. The seat is constructed from an x-frame in the fashionable, if surprising, form of ducks' heads. Constructed from ebony, decorated with gold leaf, glass, faience (a composite material made from ground quartz with alkaline glaze) and coloured glass, these richly decorated chairs affirm the regal status of Tutankhamun. Objects like these are rare and precious, museum pieces that attest to the powerful mythologies of ancient Egyptian culture.

From Egyptian times onwards, thrones have been used to single out the most prestigious members of society. During the Tang Dynasty in China (AD 618–906), chairs were adopted by the elite to mark out prestigious roles. By the time of the late Ming Dynasty (AD 1368–1644), the chair remained as a status symbol, with most of the population using stools. Whether for monarch, pope or bishop, the throne denoted authority, most notably since early examples could be

lifted up and carried, or even secured on the back of an elephant, to display the powerful individual to the assembled throngs, as a fantastic spectacle. For example, in India:

> Since their earliest contact with Europeans, Indian rulers demonstrated an interest in rare and exotic goods from the West, which were rapidly assimilated into the decoration of Indian palace interiors. Those rulers who interacted with Europeans also began to adopt aspects of Western lifestyle and behaviour, such as sitting on a chair instead of on textiles on the ground, or using a carriage instead of a palanquin.[3]

The throne of Maharaja Ranjit Singh, which dates from the early nineteenth century, represents a significant blend of Asia and Europe, the traditions of East and West. The chair is octagonal in shape, based

Maharaja Ranjit Singh's throne, early 19th century.

Chair of State and Footstool for the coronation of Charles II, 1661.

on the courtly furniture of the north Indian Mughals. The throne was created by Hafiz Muhammad Multani, a goldsmith, which is fitting since the wood and resin core is completely covered with sheets of *repoussé*, chased and engraved gold. Every inch of the surface is covered in delicate patterns, including subtle lotus flowers, symbols of purity and creation, and associated with thrones for the Hindu gods. The throne was designed to be carried in processions, and has handles on its sides for this purpose. The chair is squatter than Western examples of the time, because the maharaja would sit cross-legged on the cushion, as was the Indian custom. But the chair carried at a height in processions ensured that his royal status was confirmed.

Chairs also played a crucial role in royal events in Britain, to delineate particular roles in the ceremony of crowning the monarch, for example. The Gothic Coronation chair in Westminster Abbey is the oldest chair in England to be still used for the purpose for which it was created. Made in 1300–01 for Edward I, it has been used for the coronation of British monarchs ever since. It was decorated with plants, birds and animals by the court painter, Master Walter. A later example of a ceremonial chair is the Chair of State and Footstool used for the coronation of Charles II, created in 1661 by the royal upholsterer John Casbert for the Archbishop of Canterbury. Richly upholstered and decorated for that occasion, the chair has a beech frame and upholstered in purple velvet and a fringe of gold wire. The base is in the X-frame form, first seen in ancient Egypt and created for folding chairs. At this time, social interaction would take place in the bedchamber around the bed. Guests were received into the royal chamber and sat wherever they could, including on the floor.

The folding form of chair was used by emperors of the Ming Dynasty for the purposes of travel, either to military campaigns or to the tombs of ancestors to make sacrifices. One example, now in the collection of the Victoria & Albert Museum, was made from intricately carved lacquer on wood at the Orchard Factory in Beijing. The Chinese normally knelt on mats on the floor, and a platform arrangement was used up until the nineteenth century, to raise high-ranking officials and religious leaders above the masses during important ceremonies.

At the same time in Britain, only the most prominent figures in a domestic or royal interior would sit on a chair. As Sigfried Giedion, the modernist design theorist claimed in 1948:

> But as late as the first half of the sixteenth century, chairs are not the rule, even in the highest places. When Hans Holbein the Younger portrays Henry VIII and his privy council in 1530, his woodcut shows the members of this exalted body as tightly packed on low-back benches as were the members of the *Lit de Justice* in 1458. The unpainted, primitively joined benches, tables, and chairs found in the Alps today, or among the American colonists well into the nineteenth century, represent the domestic tradition of the late Gothic carried through the ages. Such furniture was everywhere to be found at the turn of the fifteenth century in the North as in the South. Its tradition took shape in the towns, and at the behest of burghers and patricians. It bears still the imprint of medieval austerity.[4]

For example, the Bromley-by-Bow room, which dates from 1606, and which has been preserved at the Victoria & Albert Museum, contains one carved wooden chair with a cushion on the seat, which would have been very prestigious for its occupant. The rest of the household would have sat on stools or benches against the wood-panelled wall, the lower-status seating having no backs.

It was the French court, which moved to the showplace of Versailles in 1682, that established the most intricate hierarchy expressed by means of chairs. The absolute monarch Louis XIV established the

accepted practice for behaviour at court throughout Europe in the seventeenth century. The court grew in size from 600 in 1664 to 10,000 in the late eighteenth century, after the court had moved to Versailles, and the sovereign kept order partly through the use of the chair. Only a tiny elite – including his brother, his children and grandchildren – was allowed to sit while the king was sitting, and this was only on stools. For example, in the Hall of Mirrors the 'Sun King' sat on his grand, Baroque silver throne; a canopy towered above his bewigged head, surmounted with a huge crown. The throne was placed at the top of a stepped platform to give extra height and prominence whilst the gathered assembly stood. Louis XIV also had a special wheeled chair, or *roulette*, to transport him around the huge gardens of Versailles; so again, his entourage gathered around him on foot whilst he was the only person sitting.

In the French queen's apartments, most aristocratic women were provided with cushions, or *carreaux*, on which to sit. This included the ladies-in-waiting, wives of generals and ladies of title, but not duchesses. Many preferred to stand rather than sit so low to the

Claude-Guy Hallé, *Visit of Claude-Guy Hallé to Louis XIV, Versailles*, 1685.

ground. The seating protocol was a major preoccupation of the court, and, according to Voltaire in his *Dictionnaire philosophique*:

> An armchair, a chair with a back, a stool were for many centuries important political objects and serious subjects of dispute . . . May one sit, in a particular room, on a chair or on a stool, or are we not supposed to sit at all? These were the questions that fascinated a court.[5]

Eventually, the etiquette over the use of chairs was eroded, just as the dominance of the aristocracy receded. The process was evident in the Rococo style. With the death of Louis XIV in 1715, his nephew, Philippe, duc d'Orléans, became Regent of France until Louis XV came of age. The years of the *Régence* heralded a more relaxed culture, which was reflected in the creation of the more intimate Rococo style and comparative informality. The centre of the court returned to Paris, and the most modish entertaining took place in small 'salons' rather than the overbearing grandeur of Versailles. The appearance and use of the chair became more informal. Softer, organic shapes and lighter forms were used, such as shells and vegetation, rather than heavy scrolls. This was the new age of sociability, with the salons organized by female hostesses who wielded remarkable levels of political power. Increased gender equality was marked by equality and informality in seating arrangements. More lightweight, dainty furniture was introduced, drawing inspiration from Chinese forms, and there was a revival of interest in the Gothic style. The chairs could be easily moved around the inner space of the salon to construct different groups for conversation. The French regent was a central figure in this fashion and avoided the court etiquette so rigidly applied by his uncle, and his example was later followed by Louis XV. New chair types were developed during this period, to accommodate a more relaxed pose and to aid

leisure pursuits such as reading, particularly for women. This included the *bergère*, which offered high levels of comfort with its cushions and armrests; the day bed or *chaise longue*; the *duchesse-brisée* – a *duchesse* (chaise longue) in three parts, allowing you to put your delicate, slippered feet on an upholstered, gondola chair – and the *duchesse* as a one-piece, shell-like shape, which sensually trailed the curves of the incumbent, followed in the later eighteenth century.

The fashionable salon was also in evidence in London, led by hostesses such as the Duchess of Devonshire. The rise of the European metropolis also meant that there were more public places to frequent. Sedan chairs for hire were introduced in seventeenth-century London and Paris to ferry the wealthier members of society around the dangerous and dirty city streets. Consisting of two poles either side of an

A London coffee house, c. 1700.

enclosed booth, the passenger sat within whilst they were carried by the bearers on foot. The occupants could arrange for the sedan chair to be brought into their homes and their eventual destination, so they did not have to set foot on the filthy streets at all.

While the sedan chair offered a device for exclusion and marking difference, the new London coffee houses provided a public space for men of all social classes to mingle. From the mid-seventeenth century men could meet in this public space and sit down to drink the new exotic drink of coffee, read newspapers or engage in political debate. Importantly, the seating was completely democratic and not dependent on social class or position, which was a rarity at that time. As Markman Ellis has described:

> Arriving in the coffee-house, customers were expected to take the next available seat, placing themselves next to whoever else has come before them. No seat could be reserved, no man might refuse your company. This seating policy impresses on all customers that in the coffee-house

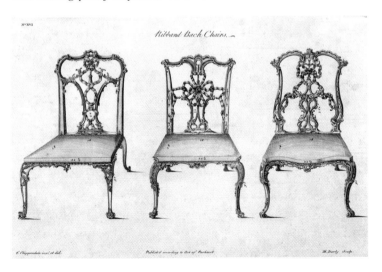

Chippendale chairs, illustrated in *The Gentleman and Cabinet-Maker's Directory*, first published in 1754.

all are equal. Though the matter of seating may appear inconsequential, the principle of equality this policy introduced had remarkable ramifications in the decades to come. From the arrangement of the chairs, the coffee-house allowed men who did not know each other to sit together amicably and expected them to converse. In the anonymous context of the city, in which most people are unknown to each other, this sociable habit was astonishing. Further more, the principle of equality established by the seating arrangements recommended equality and openness as the principle of conversation.[6]

The egalitarian conviviality of the London coffee house was reserved for men, and the leadership of style for the design of chairs was more male-dominated than was the case in eighteenth-century France. For example, the highly influential pattern book by the cabinetmaker Thomas Chippendale, *The Gentleman and Cabinet-maker's Director: Being a Large Collection of the Most Elegant and Useful Designs of Household Furniture in the Gothic, Chinese and Modern Taste,* was first published in 1754. The dominance of the male upper class was echoed in the title, and the book was even dedicated to the Duke of Northumberland. The subscribers who supported the production of the book reveal a preponderance of male aristocrats and cabinet-makers. The volume privileged the chair because examples were illustrated in line drawings right at the beginning of the plates, which also included sofas, tables and bookcases. The example of the Ribband-backed chairs shows Chippendale at his most decorative, and he was proud of these examples, explaining in the text:

> three Ribband-backed Chairs, which, if I may speak without vanity, are the best I have ever seen (or perhaps have ever been made.) The Chair on the left hand has been executed from this Design, which had an excellent effect, and gave satisfaction to all who saw it. I make no doubt

that the other two will give the same content, if properly handled in the execution. The dimensions are affixed to the design.[7]

Chairs were also privileged in another cabinetmaker's pattern book, that of George Hepplewhite, in *The Cabinet-Maker and Upholsterer's Guide* of 1788. Chairs were the first category of the volume, which was aimed at the 'mechanic and serviceable to the gentleman'.[8] Of the 125 plates, 28 were of chairs, again reinforcing their centrality to the cabinetmaker's practice.

The type of informality of the London coffee house was mirrored in early American hotels. According to one source:

> The mere idea of making a home in a hotel seemed 'little short of profanation' to the Britisher. But even worse was the notorious table d'hôte at which the Englishman was expected to dine with farmer, teamster, and his own manservant . . . Americans were by nature a

Innocent-Louis Goubaud, *The Roman Senate before Napoleon*, 1805, showing the throne-room of Napoleon I at Fontainebleau.

gregarious people who loved to live in public, to see and be seen, to hear and be heard, and to participate 'on the level'. The young American ambitious to get ahead would not dare to ask for a private room even if he wanted it; for this act would lead to the 'serious charge' that he was 'aristocratic'.[9]

But in France, the social hierarchy, partly orchestrated by the use of chairs, remained a powerful force. There was a gradual decline in the centrality of the French royal court as the European taste-maker with the ascendancy of the *bourgeois*, most obviously exemplified with the overthrow of the aristocracy at the French Revolution in 1789.

Power was soon realigned to a single autocrat in France with the self-styled emperor Napoleon, who skilfully imposed his power by using Roman, Greek and Egyptian imagery. Under the leadership of the Neo-classical painter Jacques-Louis David, the interior decorators Charles Percier and Pierre François Léonard Fontaine helped Napoleon fulfil his aspiration of using classical style to reinforce his authority. He had a number of thrones made for him, designed by Percier and Fontaine, and crafted by Georges Jacob, in the Empire style, which included gilt swags and festoons decorating a mahogany, rosewood or ebony surface. Some of the thrones were made specifically for David's studio for the grand portraits of Napoleon. Others were used for his coronation and for his royal residences. The form of the thrones was classical, with square or round backs, placed on a stepped platform with a magnificent, Roman canopy, as seen in the example of the throne-room at Fontainebleau. Like the French monarchy before him, Napoleon manipulated seating arrangements to display and impose power. Only his wife and mother were permitted to sit in armchairs in his presence and all other visitors had to sit on ordinary chairs or stools. Napoleon's foreign minister, Talleyrand, recalled a visit from the Austrian minister, Count Louis de Coblenzl, which was carefully stage-managed by Napoleon:

Bonaparte himself organised the setting. He sat at a small writing table put in a corner of an ante-chamber. All the other seats had been removed, except two sofas situated far away from the table. With only one lamp, the Austrian count came in the dimly lit room. Napoleon, standing near his table, sat down and the poor ambassador, confused, had to stand during the whole meeting.[10]

The British monarchy of the nineteenth century and the upper echelons of society emulated the French style of Louis XIV and Louis XV in the chairs they commissioned and bought to furnish royal apartments, stately homes and exclusive clubs. Queen Victoria and her beloved Prince Albert set the tone for a more domestic, relaxed and family-centred form of royal setting. The diminutive queen was always shown on a more petite chair than the ones Albert used, partly due to the fashion of that time for women, which stipulated large crinolines and voluminous skirts, making sitting on any type of armchair impossible.

The two chairs created specially for Queen Victoria and Prince Albert for the Great Exhibition held in the purpose-built 'Crystal Palace' in Hyde Park, London, in 1851 are a case in point. Made by the upholsterer Henry Eyles for show in the Furniture Section, they pay extravagant homage to the royal couple. The queen's chair is carved from walnut, with an inset porcelain plaque depicting the monarch. The seat was covered with an embroidered satin representation of the royal arms. The carved cabriole legs reveal a debt to French eighteenth-century fashion. Prince Albert's chair is 21.5 cm (8.5 in) taller and also carved from walnut. However, the much darker tone of the porcelain plaque featuring the prince and the deep red upholstery would have expressed a sense of gravitas, compared to the lightness of the queen's chair. The wide, deep, upholstered seat of the prince's chair, framed either side by heavy arms, was used for men's chairs during the mid-nineteenth century to express a certain confidence, and also the arms would restrict the female sitter, with her expansive crinoline folds. It may seem incongruous that Queen Victoria, who could count all British males as her subjects, should conform to nineteenth-century notions about gender stereotypes and the dominance of the male. However, she managed to live out a dual life as a womanly woman, wife and mother in contrast to a strong and effective head of state.[11]

As wife and mother, Queen Victoria set the tone for an ideology of feminine domesticity in Britain in the nineteenth century, and this was reflected in the design, production and use of chairs. As social relations became more complex in the dawning age of modernity, so designed spaces and objects were used to express and perform identities, particularly in relation to gender and class. The forces of modernity, particularly mechanization and the exploitation of cheap labour, made an impact on the manufacture of furniture, as with the pottery industry before it: the making of affordable furniture was based on the division of labour with one person performing a small part of the construction to speed up the process. The growing

Eugène Lami, *Reception of Queen Victoria and Prince Albert at the Château d'Eau, 3 September 1843.*

Chair made for Prince Albert for the Great Exhibition, London, 1851.

urbanization of Britain also meant that the population of towns and cities was expanding, increasing the demand for furniture and other manufactured goods, particularly amongst the middle classes. The growing labour force and increase in output made goods available to all strata of society. Therefore, the ownership and use of a chair in itself was no longer a sign of elevated status. Instead, style, materials and taste were used as important markers of identity, wealth and social standing within the context of the home. Taste in particular was debated and attempts were made to regulate it, since design commentators thought that the mass production and consumption amongst the lower classes needed addressing. This trend found particular resonance with the 'Art Furniture' movement, exemplified in particular by Charles Eastlake in his popular book *Hints on Household Taste* (1868). Based on articles the architect had written for magazines such as *The Queen* and *Cornhill Magazine*, the book promised 'to suggest some fixed principles of taste for the popular guidance of those who are not accustomed to hear such principles defined'.[12]

This kind of advice was prevalent in Victorian society, with a growing middle class eager to follow respected mores and tacitly agreed patterns of behaviour. Eastlake argued:

Our modern furniture is essentially effeminate in form. How often do we see in fashionable drawing-rooms a type of couch which seems to be composed of nothing but cushions! It is really supported by a framework of wood or iron, but this internal structure is carefully concealed by the stuffing and material with which the whole is covered. I do not wish to be ungallant in my remarks, but I fear there is a large class of young ladies who look upon this sort of furniture as 'elegant'. Now, if elegance means nothing more than a milliner's idea of the beautiful, which changes every season – so that a bonnet which is pronounced 'lovely' in 1877 becomes a 'fright' in 1878 – then no doubt this sofa, as well as a score of other articles of modern manufacture which I could mention, is elegant indeed. But, if elegance has anything in common with real beauty – beauty which can be estimated by a fixed and lasting standard – then I venture to submit that this eccentric combination of bad carpentry and bloated pillows is very *in*elegant, and, in fact, a piece of ugliness which we ought not to tolerate in our houses.[13]

A well-preserved Victorian interior can be seen at 18 Stafford Terrace, the home of the *Punch* cartoonist Linley Sambourne in west London. Furnished in the 1870s, it perfectly reflects the taste of the educated upper-middle class. The hallway is decorated in dark green wall-paper, originally William Morris *Diaper*, which can still be seen behind the many framed prints decorating the walls. The flooring is a dark brown linoleum. So the muted colours and emphasis on art reflect

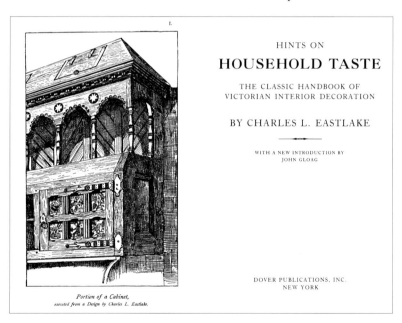

L.

HINTS ON

HOUSEHOLD TASTE

THE CLASSIC HANDBOOK OF
VICTORIAN INTERIOR DECORATION

BY CHARLES L. EASTLAKE

WITH A NEW INTRODUCTION BY
JOHN GLOAG

DOVER PUBLICATIONS, INC.
NEW YORK

Portion of a Cabinet,
executed from a Design by Charles L. Eastlake.

Frontispiece of a modern reprint of Charles Eastlake's *Hints on Household Taste,* 1868.

the type of decoration recommended by reformers such as Eastlake.

However, despite reflecting the latest critical thoughts about design reform, the gender divisions between dining room and drawing room remained firmly in place. As Juliet Kinchin has argued:

> In the nineteenth century the private interior space of the middle-class home was increasingly defined as feminine territory, the antithesis of the public, external world of work peopled by men. Within the domestic arena, however, the key rooms tended to be further grouped to either side of a male–female divide, the most explicit contrast being between the 'masculine' dining room and 'feminine' drawing room.[14]

The dining room is at the front of the house in Stafford Terrace, and the first door to lead from the hallway. In it there is an octagonal oak dining table, surrounded by eight matching chairs with dark green Moroccan leather upholstery. There are Windsor-style smoking chairs by one wall and two easy chairs by the window. This is where Linley Sambourne and his male friends would enjoy drinks and cigars after dinner. The morning room, which was adjacent to the dining room, was his wife Marion's space, with lighter furniture, including genuine eighteenth-century examples, and more upholstery and cushions, echoing Eastlake's point. The drawing room on the first floor contained a plethora of objects – framed prints and paintings on the wall, blue and white ceramics on the plate rail, a vast array of chairs in different styles and shapes. The notion that chairs in a domestic space should match in any way is a twentieth-century concept; this Victorian space was typical in that two easy chairs were placed together in a space that also included Regency and Louis XIV copies and originals in a seemingly random order. As Walter Benjamin observed about the nineteenth-century bourgeois French interior as part of his important Arcades Project:

The private individual, who in the office has to deal with reality, needs the domestic interior to sustain him in his illusions. The necessity is all the more pressing since he has no intention of allowing his commercial considerations to impinge on social ones. In the formation of his private environment, both are kept out. From this arise the phantasmagorias of the interior – which, for the private man, represents the universe. In the interior, he brings together the far away and the long ago. His living room is a box in the theatre of the world.[15]

Dining room, Linley Sambourne House, 18 Stafford Terrace, Kensington, London.

No traces remain of the furniture used by the servants, who would be mainly located in the basement, but servants would normally use less decorative chairs, including the Windsor chair or even a wooden stool. A similar identification between masculinity and the dining room was made in the painting *A Bloomsbury Family* (1907) by William Orpen. This depicts the Nicholson family, with the painter William Nicholson seated and shown in profile. He chose the decorations for the room, with its snuff-coloured walls and decorative prints. The children sit subserviently at the dining table, whilst his wife stands near the threshold of the room, almost a guest in her own domestic space.[16] As Jean Baudrillard argued in 1968 in 'Structures of Interior Design':

> The arrangement of furniture offers a faithful image of the familial and social structures of a period. The typical bourgeois interior is patriarchal; its foundation is the dining-room/bedroom combination. Although it is diversified with respect to function, the furniture is highly integrated, centring around the sideboard or the bed in the middle of the room. There is a tendency to accumulate, to fill and close off the space. The emphasis is on unifunctionality, immovability, imposing presence and hierarchical labelling.[17]

With the increase in organized public spaces in the nineteenth century, chairs were used to order the spaces, to designate places for groups and individuals. The city could be perceived as a threatening place, where strangers mingled and anything could happen. As Friedrich Engels noted about the streets in London in the 1840s:

> A town, such as London, where a man may wander for hours together without reaching the beginning of the end, without meeting the slightest hint which could lead to the inference that there is open country within reach, is a strange thing. This colossal centralization,

this heaping together of two and a half millions of human beings at one point, has multiplied the power of this two and a half millions a hundredfold; has raised London to the commercial capital of the world . . . The very turmoil of the streets has something repulsive about it – something against which human nature rebels. The hundreds of thousands of all classes and ranks crowding past each other – aren't they all human beings with the same qualities and powers, and with the same interest in being happy? And aren't they obliged, in the end, to seek happiness in the same way, by the same means? And still they crowd by one another as though they had nothing in common, nothing to do with one another, and their only agreement is the tacit one – that each keep to his own side of the pavement, so as not to delay the opposing streams of the crowd – while no man thinks to honor another with so much as a glance. The brutal indifference, the unfeeling isolation of each in his private interest becomes the more repellent and offensive, the more these individuals are crowded together within a limited space.[18]

Upper- and middle-class men no longer sought refuge in the coffee house for male bonding, but instead frequented gentlemen's clubs. One of the first to open was the Reform Club, and the seating layout was as rigid as the membership credentials. The Reform Club was opened in 1841 in an imposing Renaissance-style building with a huge central atrium designed by Charles Barry. Moroccan leather armchairs were arranged in groups around the balcony of the atrium. The Coffee House, which was in fact the restaurant, housed a series of tables with chairs arranged round them. The Club chair, with its leather-covered, plump upholstery and arms, was developed as a type during the nineteenth century and it remains in production today.

Chairs and the spaces they occupied were used to delineate society in terms of gender in the nineteenth century; they also began to be used to specify the different categories of childhood.[19] For

example, chairs were used to teach children modern manners and deportment chairs taught them how to conduct themselves. These were also known as Astley Cooper chairs, since they were created by the surgeon and anatomy expert Astley Paston Cooper (1768–1841). The height of the seat meant that children had to sit up straight, otherwise they would fall to the floor, which, given the height of the chair, would have been a terrifying experience. Cooper believed that it was healthy to teach children correct posture by making them sit bolt upright with their heads held upright. The chairs were also used to discipline unruly children, and were often placed in the corner of Victorian schoolrooms and pupils were made to sit on them

William Orpen, *A Bloomsbury Family*, 1907.

for long periods of time. In the Victorian classroom, discipline and delineations of power were also signalled by the difference between the teacher's and pupils' seats. The teacher would sit on a tall chair, behind an elevated desk, so that they could see and be seen by the entire class and reinforce their status as the controller of the space. The children sat behind desks on wooden chairs at a lower level. This

A Club chair manufactured in the early 21st century remains identical to the type developed in the late 19th century.

is a room arrangement that has persisted to the present day, perhaps less in the classroom but definitely in the lecture room and seminar spaces at universities.

In the new public space of the office, the chair was again used to delineate status and power. Office design, particularly in America, developed under the influence of Frederick Taylor's theory of scientific management. Expounded in his bestseller, *The Principles of Scientific Management* of 1911, every task was separated out and timed, to achieve ultimate efficiency – the mass-production methods of the Ford production plant were applied to the office. As Adrian Forty argued:

> Scientific management was no less partial in the advice it offered on office chairs. Clerks clearly needed the best design of chair for desk work

Child deportment chair, 1790, and a tall teacher's chair, displayed at the Wycombe Museum at High Wycombe.

and this was said to be swivel-based, with a wooden saddle seat and a slatted wooden back. If this was actually the chair that best minimized fatigue, it should have been thought equally appropriate for executives' use as well. Executives, however, were recommended to have cane seated chairs, which were said to be superior to wooden-seated ones; status debarred clerical workers from enjoying the same benefits.[20]

Chairs were also used to define power and control in other, new public areas of modernity. For example, the deckchair, an adjustable, wooden-framed seat with canvas support to sit or lie on, seems to have been first developed for the new public spaces on board ocean liners in the 1880s. This explains the original term of deck chair or the French version, *chaise transatlantique.* John Thomas Moore patented the adjustable, folding chair in 1886 and produced them in Macclesfield, Cheshire. The deckchair was also adopted for use at the seaside, an important marker of space and place for your group and belongings. The ingenious form of the deckchair, with its X-shaped, folding wooden frame, may have its roots back in the early Egyptian form of the folding stool. Evidence of these nifty stools appears on tomb paintings, and their unique form means they are lightweight and easy to manoeuvre. The X-form is decorated with duck heads, delicately inlaid in ivory, which support the leather straps that form the seat. Examples of the stools were contained in the tomb of Tutankhamun.

Later types of chairs used on ocean-liner decks include what we would now call steamer chairs, with a back support that resembled a Windsor chair and a longer frame to support the legs and feet without the canvas. Cushions would then be placed on the slatted wood for comfort. Steamer chairs were supplied on the upper-class decks of ocean liners from the late nineteenth century onwards. Their supply was limited to the upper echelons, since it presupposed enough deck space for passengers to lie and look out over the ocean, usually on the promenade deck. This was not a possibility for those thousands of passengers in steerage who had very little deck space, if any at all. Steerage would sit right below decks to eat their meals, on long wooden tables with plain chairs, fixed to the deck, as the example from the *Mauretania* in 1907 demonstrates. This space was fitted out by the shipbuilders Swan Hunter on Tyneside. By contrast, the first-class dining room was designed by high-society architect Harold Peto. This was situated on two levels, and clad in dark oak sourced from Austria, which was hand-carved; the chairs were arranged in intimate groups around hexagonal tables. Upholstered in patterned, dark pink satin, the mahogany chairs were also fixed to the deck, but this was the upper deck with the least ship movement, situated in the centre of the vessel.

The uniquely British space of the pub, or public house, presents a series of liminal and subliminal spaces that are reinforced by the introduction of chairs and seating arrangements. As Fiona Fisher has demonstrated, the Victorian pub has its roots in homes that were

Third-class restaurant on Cunard's RMS *Mauretania*, 1907.

Harold Peto, first-class restaurant, RMS *Mauretania*, 1907.

made more and more public.[21] The lower classes, including work-men, would drink in the public bar, a liminal space that could be negotiated as you stood to get served and to drink. The upper-middle classes and middle classes would be steered through special entrances to the private lounge, accessed via a separate corridor. The seating would be plusher within that area, with the invitation to create your own social grouping around a table using chairs to stake out your territory – a practice that still takes place today. Just as the deckchair is used to stake out your territory on the beach or in the park, the development of the French café followed similar lines, as Christoph Grafe has observed:

> A degree of subtle social differentiation can still be observed in many Parisian cafés while the terrace facing the street invites a mixed public ready to pay an extra charge for table service, the bar counter is the territory of the – mostly male – habitués, usually from the neighbour-hood. Often the difference between standing and sitting customers reflects social distinctions; working-class camaraderie and middle-class private respectability both have their respective territories within the same space.[22]

Whilst pubs and cafés – particularly the space around the bar – repre-sented a liminal space, the use of chairs to order and control became more prevalent in public life at the end of the nineteenth century. The theatre represents a public space that was tightly controlled by means of the patterns of seating – the private box for the upper ech-elons of society, to watch the production from their own space whilst in full view of the audience and performers. The tiers above were used for seating the next tier down of client and the stalls with the worst views for the poorest elements of the audience. The new media form of film was initially screened to vaudeville or music-hall audiences in theatres as part of the show. By the early twentieth century separate spaces were created in arcades or shops to create basic viewing theatres. These were termed nickelodeons in America and Penny-gaffs in Britain because of their cheap entrance price. In these early days the predominately working-class audience was crammed onto wooden benches with blacked-out windows. By the 1930s, and the rise of Classic Hollywood Cinema, cinema chain owners endeavoured to attract a more middle-class audience by purpose-built cinemas with plush seating, thick carpets, grand staircases and subtle lighting. The best known of these is the Odeon chain; 142 cinemas were opened under that brand name between 1930 and 1939, denoting the best of British luxury. The seats in the flagship cinema, the Odeon in London's Leicester Square, were covered in fake leopard skin. The luxury and glamour of the surroundings played a big part in the audience's lives – by 1940 there were 5,500 cinemas in Britain. There were 990 million visits to the cinema by 1940, and the average number of visits to the cinema was two per week during the 1930s. Most visitors to the cinema recall the glamour of the occasion, and as Annette Kuhn found in her oral history project about cinema attendance, more than 90 per cent of the respondents used words such as: 'comfort, space, luxury, modernity' to relive their experiences.[23]

Another public space developed in the twentieth century in the UK was the National Health Service (NHS) hospital. Established in 1948, the NHS aimed to deliver free health care to all in brand new buildings, newly furnished. The use of the chair in hospitals again reveals inbuilt hierarchies. The phrase *Take a seat* is a humane and comforting one. But in the NHS hospital or out-patient clinic, this invitation signals what could be a two- or even three-hour wait. Uncomfortable plastic chairs hold rows of anxious patients and their carers waiting to meet with consultants who perch on a bed, or rush in and out of the consulting room, or place a desk between themselves and those obliged to listen to the most devastating news. This demarcation of space extends to the ward. Doctors stand looking at the patient, lying prone. There is a hierarchy of visitors. As Blake Morrison recalled on a visit to his father in hospital:

> 'Feeling rough, Dad?' I ask.
> 'Too true.'
>
> I hug him for a moment, then slide two chairs beside the bed: a small plastic chair next to his, for me; and a slightly more comfortable armchair – actually, as minimal as that, a chair with arms – for my mother.[24]

The increasingly controlled public space of the theatre, hospital and cinema was mirrored in the private space of the domestic interior. By the 1930s the three-piece suite – a couch able to accommodate two or three people, plus two single easy chairs – was predominant. This was partly as a result of the increased suburbanization of Britain, particularly in the south of England. These arrangements reinforced the hierarchies within the heterosexual, nuclear family:

> Whatever it was that went to make the lower-working-class home 'cosy', parents had first, often sole, rights in it. They took, of course, the best bed and bedding and the two cushioned armchairs nearest the fire. In some families children were forbidden to sit on these at any time; during parental absence they had to remain vacated thrones of power.[25]

The British playwright Harold Pinter explored power relations within the family in *The Homecoming* (1965). Essentially a portrayal of family as predator, the chair features as a confirmation of the status of the father. When Max's eldest son, Teddy, returns late one night with his wife, Ruth, to the family home in England, Teddy ushers her into the living room:

Ruth: Can I sit down?

Teddy: Of course.

Ruth: I'm tired.

Pause.

Teddy: Then sit down.

She does not move.

   That's my father's chair.

Ruth: That one?

Teddy: (*smiling*) Yes, that's it.[26]

In the 1973 Peter Hall film of the scene, Ruth sits on the sofa, acknowledging the power of the absent patriarch. Similarly, Jonathan Franzen in his novel *The Corrections* (2001) described the power of the chair to represent its owner:

> To the west of the Ping-Pong table was Alfred's great blue chair. The chair was overstuffed, vaguely gubernatorial. It was made of leather, but it smelled like the inside of a Lexus . . . [W]hen Alfred retired from the Midland Pacific Railroad, he set about replacing the old cow-smelling black leather armchair in which he watched TV and took his naps. He wanted something really comfortable, of course, but after a lifetime of providing for others he needed more than just comfort: he needed a monument to this need. So he went, alone, to a non-discount furniture store and picked out a chair of permanence. An engineer's chair. A chair so big that even a big man got lost in it; a chair designed to bear up under heavy stress.[27]

And the American historian Leora Auslander described the power of the chair to represent its owner, skillfully drawing on life writing:

> I choose a chair. I take that chair home. Over the next months and years

guests respond to me and to my chair, some seeing in it one thing, some another. They cannot see in it what I hoped for them to see because what I hoped was itself necessarily contradictory and occluded. They respond with their interpretations of my chair and me. I respond and am changed by their responses. I have been made by that chair and I have made the chair. The chair was full of meanings over which I had no control, and of which I had only partial knowledge when I acquired it. In my home it acquired new meanings.[28]

The most obvious case of a chair being used to objectify and suppress a victim is the electric chair. This was a specially constructed wooden chair to which the prisoner was strapped and put to death by electrocution by means of electrodes on the body. It was first introduced in 1890 in the United States, since it was thought to be cleaner and more efficient than hanging. It is still legal in some states, but is very rarely used, having being replaced now by the lethal injection. Thomas Edison was opposed to its creation, because he feared it would undermine the image he was trying to create of electricity as safe for use in the home. This ultimate symbol of control and discipline entered the cultural landscape when Andy Warhol worked with the haunting image of an empty electric chair from 1963 onwards in his screen-printing work, the last execution by electric chair in New York state taking place that same year.

Therefore, from a regal symbol of authority over one's subjects, even in the afterlife in ancient Egyptian times, the chair has been transformed over the intervening 3,000 years into the ultimate symbol of repression and objectification. The complex relationship between modern designer and the chair will be considered next; a relationship that still revolves around power relationships.

A prisoner is prepared for execution in 'Old Sparky', Sing-Sing Prison's infamous electric chair. Photograph taken c. 1900 by William M. Van der Weyde.

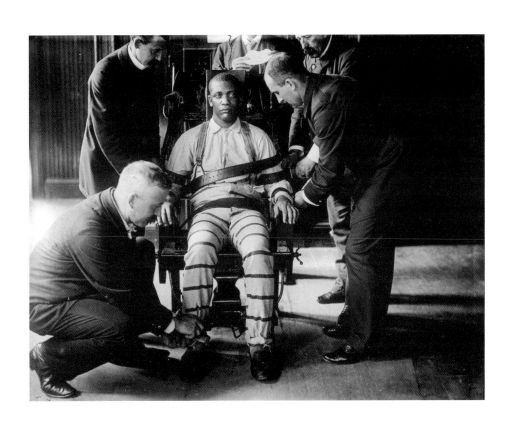

2 The Designer's Presence

Since ancient Egyptian times the chair has worked as an important marker of territory, space and status. It has been used to signal superiority and prestige in terms of position, power and social rank. A more recent development of this meaning has been its close association with the modernist designer. Because the chair is so closely associated with the body and with performing particular roles, it has been adopted by modern architects to represent their aesthetic credo. It is the essence of the designer, represented in three dimensions, often using innovative technology and construction. Ownership of the exclusive and genuine designer chair can confer status on the owner and/or user, and the original power comes from the association with the star designers themselves. Like the apprentice's model, the chair design is the ultimate design statement, the essence of a design world view. As one style commentator, Peter York, noted: 'Chairs have become the designers' dissertation.'[1] And we like to associate classic chair forms with named designers, almost as if the chair were a child or a pet. Pity anybody who messes with the familiar classic original, even if it's the designers themselves!

Here is just one example in *Design* magazine from 1970, commenting on the British designer Robert Heritage's copies of the popular dining chair he designed for the liner *QE2*:

Robert Heritage, detail of Q Range chair, 1969. Aluminium alloys are bonded together using epoxy adhesive, a technical innovation for the British furniture industry.

Race Furniture Ltd have just launched a contract range of free-standing and linked seating and tables, called the Q-range, designed by Robert Heritage on the lines of his *QE2* dining chair.

The Apollo . . . a conference chair, is a disappointingly modified version of Heritage's original design for the *QE2*. It has a simpler canti-levered backrest which dispenses with the vertical plywood shell, and a horizontal instead of upward-curving seat.[2]

The chair has come to be intimately linked with its designer, and the notion of the authentic and the copy is vital when it comes to modern chair design. Like the cheap copy, we are now living in the age of the knock-off, designer reproduction chair, exemplified in ads such as these. The Eames armchair is used to advertise Sony televisions and the image decorates drink coasters sold by the Museum of

Robert Heritage, Q Range, 1970. Prototype chair on display at the Design Centre, London, 1968, in a mock-up of a corner of the Britannia Restaurant for the *QE2*.

Modern Art (MoMA) in New York. This fetishization of the modernist, iconic chair rests on the figure of the celebrity designer and the notion of the real and the copy. The built-in tension between the one-off work of art and the mass-produced object is crucial to twentieth-century modernism as a whole. As Rosalind Krauss has argued, the original can be an original only in the context of mass production, it is 'necessary to the concept of the original, the spontaneous, the new'.[3] The chair as a unique work of art holds this power of representation only as it exists in the context of cheap, mass-produced chairs. One high-end furniture manufacturer, Knoll, bought the rights to the formal registered trademark status of several of Ludwig Mies van der Rohe chairs of 1929, including the 'Barcelona Chair'. Other furniture makers are allowed to produce copies of the chair, so long as they don't call it by its official title. As part of its marketing strategy, Knoll stamps Mies's signature on the base of the chair and issues a certificate of authenticity. The company also pays a levy to MoMA.[4] This demonstrates that the designer chair survives as an 'authentic' artwork, and its power is reinforced by the availability of cheap copies.

This chapter looks at the emergence and changing meaning of the designer chair over time. It is about the designer chair as a metaphor for the designer, and how this metaphor came to change from the late nineteenth century, when the modern designer chair first came into being, up until the present day, when its power has been further bolstered by the cheap copy and endless repetition in the media.

Modern architects conventionally designed furniture for their own buildings. Perhaps this was to ensure complete control over the interior space, to order and arrange the inhabitants within. The most famous pieces of furniture designs and the most prolific ones have been designs for the chair. In ideal representations of these interiors, whether architectural perspectives or public relations photographs, 'the chairs . . . often serve as "stand-ins" – or rather "sit-ins" – for human beings, representing "abstracts" of the bodies which are presumably intended to use and inhabit them".[5]

When we look at modern designer chairs at the moment when they were first produced, the chair acted almost as a metaphor for the potential user. But later on, by means of museum collections and displays as well as exhibitions, the chairs came to be interpreted as standing for the presence of the designer. The chair stood in for the presence of its creator, whether in a domestic setting, as a crucial part of a public environment, such as the office, or in museum displays. These chairs were often inserted into spaces that were highly visible and public, spaces with huge glass curtain walls and open-plan interiors. The physical presence of the designer was therefore inserted into the space through the metaphor of the chair. And this is usually a space that the architect has also designed. With the profusion of copies of designer chairs, the status of these objects becomes even more elevated.

The chair was used by modern architects to order and define how their buildings would be used and, in a broader sense, what their design philosophy was. As the architect and Independent Group theorist Peter Smithson argued in 1986:

> It could be said that when we design a chair, we make a society and a city in miniature. Certainly, this has never been more obvious than in this century. One has a perfectly clear notion of the sort of city, and the sort of society envisaged by Mies van der Rohe, even though he has never said much about it. It is not an exaggeration to say that the Miesian city is implicit in the Mies chair.[6]

This was a process that can be traced back to the nineteenth century with the Arts and Crafts Movement. The first example of a chair to be produced by Morris & Co. was the Sussex chair designed in 1860,

Sussex chair, Philip Webb, 1860.

so-called because it was based on rural examples seen in the eponymous county by the firm's business manager, George Warrington Taylor. The naming of the chair is significant, since the philosophy of the Arts and Crafts Movement, driven by Marxist William Morris, was to return to the pre-industrial values of a bygone age, when chairs were created individually by hand, using simple construction techniques. Of course, this was an illusion, since the Sussex chair was designed by the architect Philip Webb, and its dainty turned form in beech was produced on a large scale until the early twentieth century. Its simple, rush seating symbolized rural authenticity. It was such a commercial success that an entire Sussex range was created of corner chairs, children's chairs and settles, selling for 7 shillings in 1912. The chair is an early example of a designer object being used to frame the potential user, because it was used by Jane and William Morris for the Red House in Kent, designed for them by Webb in 1859.

The chair was the architect's vision of architecture condensed in a chair. The Red House was a Gesamtkunstwerk, with every piece of decoration reinforcing the Arts and Crafts message, from the

Sussex chairs *in situ*, the hall of Kelmscott Manor.

hand-embroidered hangings and the Gothic-style wooden cabinets to the hand-knotted rugs. Morris also used the chairs in his Hammersmith home in west London and his summer retreat at Kelmscott Manor, Oxfordshire. Kelmscott's sparse hall shows the chairs in situ, complemented by Morris & Co.'s Strawberry Thief chintz, oak chairs and table, decorated with eight table mats embroidered by May Morris (William Morris's daughter) in the 1920s. The Sussex chair was a chair with a message: it created an upright posture in the sitter, and a quiet, rustic simplicity in the interior. However, the Sussex chair was designed as an occasional chair, not for lounging but for dining. Far more comfortable and luxurious was the Adjustable chair. Again, the prototype was seen by Taylor in Sussex, who sent a

Adjustable chair, Philip Webb, 1876–90.

sketch to Webb in 1866. Webb created the design for the chair, which was produced by the firm from 1869 onwards and became one of its most popular designs. More relaxing than the Sussex chair, it could be used for the languid poses favoured by the Pre-Raphaelites, and was demonstrated by Jane Morris.

The chair continued to be used by designers and architects to determine the aesthetic ambience of their interiors as the nineteenth century drew to a close. The side chair designed by the Arts and Crafts architect, and founder of the Century Guild, Arthur Heygate Mackmurdo is an architect's statement suspended in wood. This conventionally shaped chair dating from 1883 is personalized by a carved Art Nouveau back in Honduras mahogany, with waving tendrils, almost like fronds of seaweed. The chair was produced by furniture manufactures Collinson & Lock for the dining room of the Century Guild headquarters, and it is one of the first examples of Art Nouveau applied to the chair. However, it is only the back that is stylized, and set into the eighteenth-century form of the chair. Art Nouveau by the turn of the century touched all parts of the chair, with tendrils wrapping round chair legs and the form almost melting into the carpet beneath.

Like William Morris, the Belgian Art Nouveau designer Henry Van de Velde built a new home for himself and his new bride, complete with all furnishings, in 1895. The Villa Bloemenwerf in Uccle, a suburb of Brussels, was built to vernacular design with dining-room chairs that built upon Arts and Crafts examples. The pale ash was styled in more elegant, curved forms, sinuous and lightweight, but the rush seats were a rustic echo of the Sussex chair. Made with and without arms, the chairs were subsequently produced for Van de Velde's clients in more expensive materials, including padouk, mahogany and oak with leather or cloth seats.

Jane Morris as posed by Rossetti at his Cheyne Walk flat, photograph attributed to John R. Parsons, 1865.

Similar control over the entire interior was used by Victor Horta, particularly in the design of his own house in the Ixelles area of Brussels in 1898. The dining room features a set of six chairs in light oak, which fit seamlessly into the space, with its glazed white brick faced walls, carved oak cupboards and dining table. Horta, as the architect of his own home, designed the entire setting in which the chairs functioned. Belgian Art Nouveau then made an impact in France, with Hector Guimard visiting Horta from Paris in 1895, and drawing upon his influences. He returned to Paris to design the famous Metro signs in metalwork, trained into tortuous shapes and organic forms with lights that resembled exotic plants. Guimard also designed a complete building and interior at the Castel Béranger apartments, Rue La Fontaine, built in the years 1895–7. In the Art Nouveau spirit, everything

Charles Rennie Mackintosh and Margaret MacDonald, Ladies' Luncheon Room from Miss Cranston's Tea Rooms, Ingram Street, Glasgow, c. 1900, reconstructed in Kelvingrove Art Gallery and Museum, Glasgow.

was coordinated, the chairs, tables, even doorknobs harmonizing in a fluid, asymmetrical whole. The chairs were placed within the slightly disturbing interiors, a part of the overwhelming ensemble.

This was also the period when chairs featured as part of room sets in the many international design exhibitions. These room sets usually included chairs as symbols of inhabitation, an invitation to fantasize about being part of the designer's vision. Georges Hoentschel's Salon des Eglantiers was displayed in the decorative art pavilion at the Exposition Universelle (World Fair) in Paris in 1900. The interior consisted of carved, mirrored panels featuring a wild rose motif. This was also used on the mahogany chairs, with tendrils and leaves writhing around the chairs' legs and arms.

Charles Rennie Mackintosh used the form of the chair to great effect for the tea rooms and homes he designed. The high-back chairs

Dining room by Frank Lloyd Wright, Francis W. Little House, Wayzata, Minnesota, 1912–14.

he designed for the Argyle Street Tea Rooms in Glasgow – and then used in his own Glasgow home – lack the rural charm of Morris. The extremity of the high backs serves to create an intimate space around a table, screening the occupants off from the rest of the interior. The height of the chair back (136 cm / 54 in) is accentuated by the low seat height, and these drawn-out proportions were echoed throughout Mackintosh's interiors, with linear painted decoration and patterned carpets. The chair unites the ensemble and displays the users of the chair as part of the designer's overall vision.

This was an approach also taken by the Wiener Werkstätte, a group of architects, artists and designers who were greatly influenced by Mackintosh's aesthetic. Founded in Vienna in 1903, the group not only designed chairs and interiors, but clothing as well. Its first commission was for the Purkersdorf Sanatorium, built in 1904–5. Its architect, Josef Hoffmann, oversaw the project, designing chairs based on the cube of the main entrance, which harmonized with the geometric patterns on the floor and wall. The company has been resurrected, and chairs are now offered for sale by the Vienna-based company Neue Wiener Werkstätte at a premium, earned by the historic credentials of the original group. Such perfectly coordinated interiors, with the chair taking centre stage for the designed occupant, was a hallmark of the Wiener Werkstätte, as it was for the American architect Frank Lloyd Wright. Again, the architect takes control of the entire open-plan environment, ensuring, for example, that the inhabitants of his Prairie House, built in 1909, sit on chairs that echo the horizontals and verticals of the interior in blond oak.

The design vision of the Modern Movement echoed the *Gesamtkunstwerk* of the earlier Arts and Crafts and Art Nouveau avant-garde, but the style and materials used were far more radical. The Modern Movement abandoned wood in favour of metal, and more open, skeletal designs replaced the detailed patterns of textiles or carving. But the aim remained unchanged: to order the very public interior spaces of the modernist buildings and their inhabitants, using the design and careful placing of chairs. A prime example is the German Pavilion in Barcelona, designed by Mies van der Rohe. He designed the chair with his long-term partner and collaborator Lilly Reich, and designed interiors and furniture only with her, never alone. Following his move to America in 1938, he did not come up with any new furniture designs; the Barcelona chair remains his most famous work. In 1957 he stated that 'A chair is a very difficult object. A skyscraper is almost easier. That is why Chippendale is famous.'[7]

Designed for the International Exhibition in Barcelona of 1929, the Pavilion was constructed from luxurious materials including shimmering gold, marble and shiny brass. The simple structure was virtually not an interior at all, with the space encased in huge swathes of plate glass, framed in metal. Erected to house the official opening ceremony conducted by the Spanish king, Alfonso XIII, and his queen, Victoria Eugenie, the two Barcelona chairs and their matching footstools dominate the deserted space. Placed on a black carpet, the chairs were constructed from chromium-plated steel in a complex arrangement that was bolted together in early examples. The padded pig skin-covered cushions rest on leather straps. Although isolated in the space against the onyx dore marble wall, and the ornamental pool outside, the chairs are larger than life. The perfectly matched proportions of 75 cm (30 in) for depth, height and length are much more imposing than the average chair at some 50 cm (20 in) wide. The chair was also extremely heavy and could not be easily manoeuvred around the space. Based on the Roman X-chair, the Barcelona chairs have obvious regal connotations, although it is debatable whether the Spanish royal couple ever actually sat on them. The Barcelona chair went into commercial production immediately and was redesigned by Mies van der Rohe in 1950, after Lilly Reich had died, using the new material of stainless steel with the less expensive upholstery of cow leather.

Mies van der Rohe used his signature chair in later interiors, including the Tugendhat House in Brno, Czechoslovakia, in 1930. With Lilly Reich he also designed the special Tugendhat chairs for the living area in tubular steel with silver-grey fabric, and the cantilevered, Brno chair in chromium-plated, tubular steel with white calfskin or red velvet upholstery. Like in the Barcelona Pavilion, the chairs dominated the sparsely furnished space. The main area was divided only by a semicircular Macassar ebony screen and marble partition. The flooring was white linoleum and the ceilings completely plain. The chairs echo the emptiness of the interior space, with their minimal, metal construction and empty volume around the cantilever legs, a space normally cluttered by four legs or dense upholstery. The chairs appear to be weightless, surrounded by as much space as possible, much like the building itself.

Demonstrating similar qualities of space and weightlessness was the Wassily chair by Mies van der Rohe's Bauhaus colleague Marcel Breuer. Breuer was inspired by his newly purchased Adler bicycle to use tubular steel for the design of a chair. He approached Adler, who were not interested in the concept, and so developed his prototype with the tubular-steel manufacturer Mannesmann Steel Works and the aid of a plumber. Writing two years after the design was finalized, he stated:

> Two years ago, when I saw the finished version of my first steel club armchair, I thought that this out of all my work would bring me the most criticism. It is my most extreme work both in its outward appearance and in the use of materials; it is the least artistic, the most logical, the least 'cosy' and the most mechanical.[8]

Mies van der Rohe, Barcelona chair, 1929.

And the chair is not welcoming: if you do sit on it you are tilted back at an unfamiliar angle, your knees are lifted up, and your back is also angled at a backward tilt. A contemporary image of one of the first prototypes showed a masked female Bauhaus student perched on the seat, the faceless woman emphasizing the mechanical look of the chair. This portrait of the young designer on the chair, on the other hand, in relaxed pose, simply highlights the object's modernity.

Breuer marketed the chair through a firm he founded with Kalman Lengyel, Standard-Möbel, rather than through the Bauhaus itself. The chair featured in numerous modernist interiors, including the living room for Walter Gropius's house for the Weissenhofsiedlung in 1927, when it was matched with a tubular steel side chair and day bed. The chairs were also used in the newly built Masters' dwellings at the Bauhaus, and this is where the title originally came from – at first it was called the B3, since Breuer's original range was all prefixed with a 'B'. There was a folding version of the chair, B4, which was included in one of the Gropius Weissenhofsiedlung houses. The lightness of construction was an important part of Breuer's aesthetic, in direct opposition to Mies van der Rohe's throne-like Barcelona chair. Breuer was also centrally involved in the development of the cantilever chair, the original conception being credited to Mark Stam.[9] The radical move from four legs to the cantilever structure added to the air of weightlessness and space created by tubular steel furniture generally. It aided in decluttering the modern interior, allowing a freer appreciation of the surroundings. A complex legal battle over the copyright for the designs of Breuer's tubular steel furniture erupted when he moved manufacturing operations from Standard-Möbel to Thonet. The owner of Standard-Möbel eventually successfully sued Thonet for the ownership of royalties on all cantilever chairs. It was not until 1960 that Breuer was able to produce his original designs under the name of Cesca, his daughter's name.

Marcel Breuer seen here on his Wassily chair, 1925.

Like Mies van der Rohe, the modernist architect Le Corbusier worked closely with a female collaborator, Charlotte Perriand, to produce iconic chair designs. Le Corbusier was excessively concerned with space, cleanliness and order. His designs for private residences, such as the Villa Savoye at Poissy (1929–31), featured a perfectly white-stuccoed exterior, sweeping interior spaces and extensive open-plan arrangements around minimal fixtures and fittings. Charlotte Perriand joined his practice in 1927 and developed three chairs for his design projects at the time. The B301 sling-back chair was designed to enhance conversation. Constructed from tubular steel with leather straps for armrests, it had a seat and back made from animal skin. One of the principal designs was the Grand Confort. This consisted of a tubular steel frame which cradled leather-covered, soft cushions. The B306 chaise longue was also designed at this time. Le Corbusier and Charlotte Perriand's furniture designs were displayed at the Salon d'Automne in 1929 in the 'One-Room Flat'. His cousin, Pierre Jeanneret, was also credited with the designs, although it is more likely that he mainly oversaw the business side of things. The furniture was displayed on a green glass floor, which was illuminated, enhancing the luminosity of the green glass table. Around the table were placed four B302 swivel chairs in black leather and chrome. For Le Corbusier, chairs were equipment for houses, which in themselves were 'machines for living in'. Writing in *Vers une architecture* (Towards a New Architecture) in 1923, he declared:

> If we eliminate from our hearts and minds all dead concepts in regard to the houses and look at the question from a critical and objective point of view, we shall arrive at the 'House Machine', the mass-production house, healthy (and morally so too) and beautiful in the same way that the working tools and instruments which accompany our existence are beautiful.[10]

However, whilst this may have been Le Corbusier's intention – and his and Perriand's work was used to establish the architect's presence in many of his later designs – the architect-designed chair began to shift in meaning in the years leading up to and just after the Second World War. Designers like Charles and Ray Eames were first and foremost designers of furniture, and secondly architects. They did not design chairs to occupy buildings they had designed, but created them as stand-alone objects, almost like pieces of sculpture. The chairs did not echo the transparency of the modernist home, but had a presence in the 1950s open-plan interior. Something happened to make the chair stand as a metaphor for the actual designer. This trend began when the chair started to be regarded as an artwork in its own right.

Le Corbusier, Pierre Jeanneret and Charlotte Perriand, LC3 *Grand Confort* lounge chair, 1928. Cassina I Maestri.

This transformation was not initiated by the designers themselves; it was a process mainly initiated by museums and galleries, often in conjunction with furniture manufacturers and distributors. The start of the change can be tracked back to the Museum of Modern Art's exhibition 'Cubism and Abstract Art' organized by Alfred H. Barr Jr in 1936, which exhibited the Red/Blue chair by Gerrit Rietveld, lent to the museum by Alexander Calder, the sculptor. The chair itself is an experimental prototype, based on the De Stijl aesthetic of minimizing visual form to verticals and horizontals using a restricted colour palette. It was from here that it became the 'icon' of De Stijl, postdating the movement by some twenty years. It was also from this point onwards that the chair began to stand in for the designer.

The development of modernism in America, and New York in particular, as explored by Serge Guilbaut in his excellent book *How New York Stole the Idea of Modern Art* (1983), has illuminated the annexing of modernism on behalf of America and American institutions. Whilst Guilbaut explored this tendency in terms of fine art, it also applies to design and architecture, and had begun with the opening of MoMA in New York. Here, for the first time, designer chairs were arranged in an orderly procession – a trend that has continued until the present day. MoMA's Curatorial Department for Architecture and Design was founded in 1932, and was the first one of its kind to display architecture and design from around the world. By showing the chairs as representations of the designers – on display in neat rows just like paintings, idealized on the museum's walls – it also annexed the designers themselves. It is worth noting that currently nearly one quarter of MoMA's online highlights of the architecture and design collection is made up of chairs.

If this was the starting point, how and why did it progress? Efforts to make design the same as fine art, to make it as important, led to attempts to treat it almost like sculpture and to be at pains to link an object with its creator, presenting it in pristine condition on a plinth, without anybody sitting on it. The chair was the perfect object to use for this purpose. It became divorced from the original interior space it was designed for, and started being seen as a stand-alone art object.

The furniture displays at MoMA furthered this trend, with the 'Good Design' shows of the 1950s to which crucial designers such as Charles and Ray Eames contributed. MoMA also organized the 'Design for Use, USA' travelling exhibition shown at Stuttgart in Germany (1951–2), which was essentially part of the Marshall Plan and the spread of Cold War culture; the exhibition 'Fifty Years of American Art' of 1955 held in Paris and elsewhere in Europe also included contemporary American chairs.[11] Hence, in New York, modernist design was officially supported and the designers were constructed as fine artists and enlisted to serve in the Cold War, with Charles and Ray Eames at the forefront.

Charles Eames and Eero Saarinen had designed furniture for the Department of Industrial Design at MoMA's exhibition 'Organic Design in Home Furnishings' competition in 1940. As part of the ensemble the pair designed a soft, sculpted and upholstered side chair and curved armchair that won first prize in both categories of case and seat furniture. Constructed from moulded plywood, the furniture was technically innovative and introduced the latest breakthrough in automobile manufacturing to the construction of the chair. Mass production of the chairs proved challenging, and the process was hampered by the USA's entry into the Second World War. However, the form of the chairs inspired later Eames designs, particularly the plastic shell (1950), the wire shell (1952), the La Fonda chair (1961) and the Soft Pad chair (1960).[12] The Eameses' work continued to be displayed at MoMA, with exhibitions including 'Design for Use' (1944), 'New Furniture Designed by Charles Eames' (1946) and 'The International Competition for Low-Cost Furniture' (1948). The Eameses characterized American Cold War culture in their innovative use of high technology and new materials. The moulded seat part of the armchair designed for the 1948 competition was constructed from neoprene-coated aluminium, supported on a metal frame with wooden runners. MoMA funded the product development of the chair, and it was eventually manufactured by Herman Miller and Zenith Plastics in fibreglass, supported on a more traditional wood and metal frame. In 1950 the Eames armchair went into production, and also entered MoMA's permanent collection. The modernist room settings of the 1946 exhibition, and the subsequent marginalization of Ray until recently, confirmed Charles Eames as a twentieth-century, modernist hero designer.

The Eameses' bestselling chair was the Lounge chair with matching ottoman. Constructed from moulded plywood that was veneered in rosewood with leather upholstery, the chair was manufactured and marketed by Herman Miller. Selling at $404 (approximately £145) in 1956, it was an expensive, luxury item. Its popularity, however, was enduring, and the company sold 100,000 pieces in 1975, yielding $100 million (approximately £40 million) in retail sales.[13] Proof of its continued status as a design classic is its starring role in the American television comedy *Frasier*. To Frasier's perpetual frustration, his father, a working-class, retired cop, favours his own scruffy La-Z-Boy lounger to the designer classic, which is poised, unoccupied, at the back of the set for much of the time. The chair is designed very definitely for lounging, for leaning back, feet on the matching stool to watch television or to read. Resting your body on the leather-covered duck feathers, down and foam you are cradled by this quintessential, modern designer couple, safe in the knowledge that you have taste, style and status.

Other designers who were part of the clique and who met as students at Cranbrook Academy of Art, Michigan, along with the

The Herman Miller-manufactured Eames Lounge chair seen here in production.

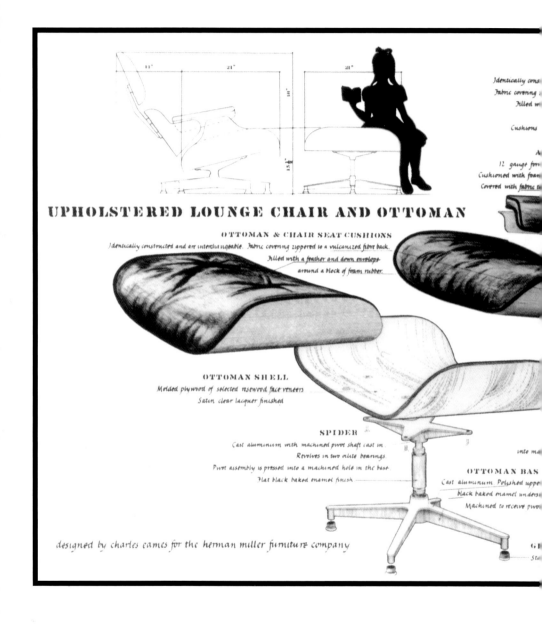

UPHOLSTERED LOUNGE CHAIR AND OTTOMAN

OTTOMAN & CHAIR SEAT CUSHIONS

Identically constructed and are interchangeable. Fabric covering zippered to a vulcanized fibre back.
Filled with a feather and down envelope
around a block of foam rubber.

OTTOMAN SHELL

Molded plywood of selected rosewood face veneers
Satin clear lacquer finished

SPIDER

Cast aluminum with machined pivot shaft cast in
Revolves in two mitre bearings
Pivot assembly is pressed into a machined hole in the base
Flat black baked enamel finish

Identically const
Fabric covering
Filled wi

Cushions

12 gauge form
Cushioned with foam
Covered with fabric t

into ma

OTTOMAN BAS

Cast aluminum Polished upper
black baked mamel undersi
Machined to receive pivo

designed by charles eames for the herman miller furniture company

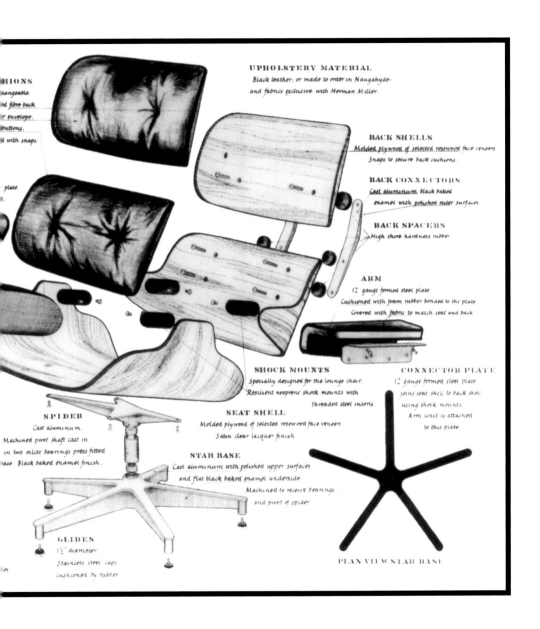

Charles and Ray Eames, Lounge chair and ottoman, 1956. Herman Miller ad featuring an exploded diagram of its complex construction.

Eameses include the architect Eero Saarinen, who designed the Tulip chair, and Florence Knoll, founder with her husband of Knoll Associates Inc. in 1946. Unlike the Eameses, Saarinen was less concerned with the technology and construction of the chair, and more focused on the overall initial impact of a unified whole. The Tulip chair was constructed from a coated light metal base and moulded seat in polyester with a loose cushion. Without the clutter of four separate legs, or exposed, complex metal supports, the chair is ideal for dining in any modernist home. The metal construction is hidden beneath the white, synthetic coating. The perfection and smoothness of the form has made the chair a perennial bestseller for Knoll. Marketed as part of KnollStudio's Saarinen Collection, the Tulip chair 'reflects the KnollStudio commitment to timeless, enduring design . . . and confirm[s] [its] unwavering belief in the power and utility of modern design.'[14] Knoll celebrated the fiftieth anniversary of the design of the Tulip chair by offering a commemorative medallion and special certificate of authenticity with every purchase from the Tulip collection in 2007 and 2008. This reinforced the image of the chair as an artwork, providing proof of authenticity as would a limited edition of fine art prints. The chair is still available with or without arms; swivel or static; in black, the original white, and platinum for just under £1,000 or $1,100 for the genuine Knoll article, depending on the finish selected. Copies retail for £2,000–£3,000, or $3,000–$4,000.

The authentic Womb chair by Saarinen is even more expensive at £2,553 or $3,800. Sleek and uncluttered, it offers an upholstered refuge and more relaxed posture than the Tulip upright chair. It was originally commissioned by Florence Knoll, who wanted 'a chair that was like a basket full of pillows . . . something [she] could curl up in'.[15] Created in upholstered latex foam on a fibreglass, reinforced plastic shell, supported by slim, chrome-plated steel rod legs and base, the chair was bought by MoMA for its permanent

Florence Knoll and Eero Saarinen with the Tulip chair, 1956.

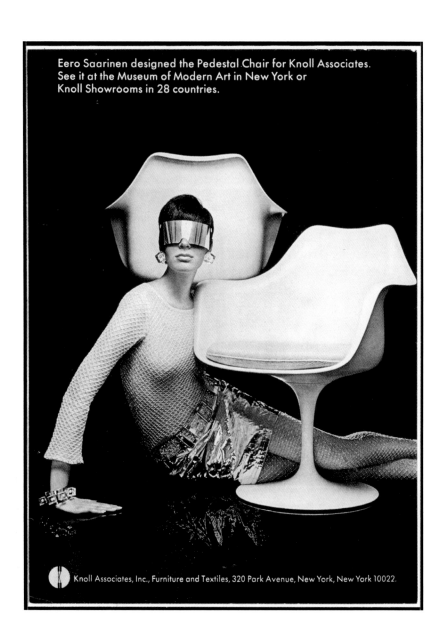

Eero Saarinen designed the Pedestal Chair for Knoll Associates.
See it at the Museum of Modern Art in New York or
Knoll Showrooms in 28 countries.

Knoll Associates, Inc., Furniture and Textiles, 320 Park Avenue, New York, New York 10022.

collection in 1946 and was used in touring exhibitions to spread the Cold War message.

Also manufactured by Knoll were the wire chairs designed by the sculptor Harry Bertoia. Here the chair operates almost like a piece of fine art, elegant and sculptural with the emphasis on shaping the chromium-plated, round bar steel into a fluid diamond shape, with curved armrests. The cushion was the only concession made to comfort, and these chairs were created more to impress guests in a modernist home, or to grace the plinths of the museum, rather than function as a seat. Chairs from this period of American post-war design history were created as individual objects, stand-ins for the designers, but designed to fit into any modernist space. This differed from the first modernist stage, where architects originally designed chairs for a specific context, usually for a building they had designed. The American chairs functioned as official symbols of high culture, to symbolize the nation's modernist design credentials as part of the Cold War offensive. By contrast, in the austere years of wartime and early post-war Britain the chair was used as part of the creation of a particularly British national identity, mainly for the domestic market, through the propaganda of the 'good design' movement of the Utility Design Scheme (1942–52).

The Utility Design Scheme prolonged the influence of Morris and the Arts and Crafts ambience, with cosy wood and Cotswold styling. Introduced by the Board of Trade in 1942, the scheme addressed the problem of furniture production at a time of an acute shortage of materials and labour. The designer and furniture manufacturer Gordon Russell headed the Board of Trade Utility Furniture Design Panel to select the approved designs: 'I felt that to raise the whole standard of furniture for the mass of people was not a bad war job.'[16] The first range of this worthy scheme was designed by Edwin Clinch and Herbert Cutler and consisted of two bedroom suites, two dining-room suites

A futuristic-looking ad from Knoll International for the futurist-looking Tulip chair.

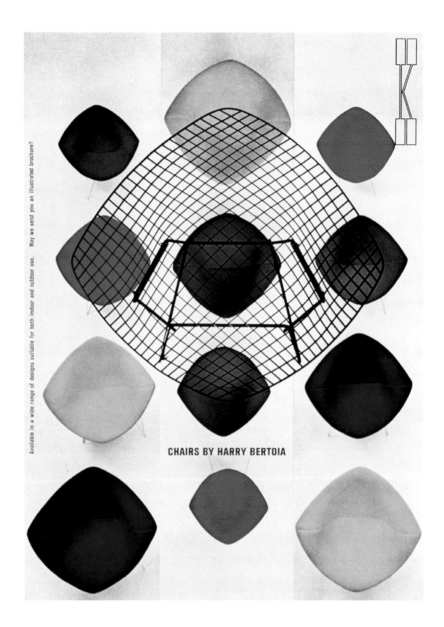

CHAIRS BY HARRY BERTOIA

and two easy chairs, largely inspired by the Arts and Crafts Movement and the authentic Windsor chair. The ladder-backed dining chairs in oak were solid and sensible, the easy chair frugal with narrow wooden arms. Exhibited at the Building Centre in London, late in 1942, the Chiltern range received a mixed reception. The metropolitan middle-class public admired it, but others would have preferred something more decorative and ostentatious.[17] The range of furniture was made available, through a coupon scheme, only to newly weds and those families who had been bombed out of their homes. It was made under licence, eventually by 150 firms, in a series of zones, to ensure the most economical use of fuel and materials. The items were numbered to indicate which range and locality they came from. In 1946 the more upmarket and expensive Cotswold range was introduced and featured at the Council of Industrial Design's exhibition at the V&A Museum, 'Britain Can Make It'. The show's title was based on a British wartime propaganda film, *Britain Can Take It*, and was organized to present contemporary British design with an eye to stimulating exports. It featured room settings for a range of social classes, from coal miners to television commentators, and many examples of Utility furniture. There were other chairs on display, for example, the leading British furniture designer Ernest Race exhibited a dining chair constructed from aluminium with rubber cushioning for the seat and back. But the visitors in general were disappointed by the dreariness of the exhibits and the predominance of Utility. In 1948 the scheme was withdrawn as part of the new 'Freedom to Design' initiative, but remained popular, since it did not attract purchase tax. The Utility scheme has more recently been reappraised by design historians as a positive contribution in terms of sustainability. Simple, solid and well made from locally sourced materials, the scheme did engender an awareness of the entire product life cycle, and many pieces remain in use today.[18]

Harry Bertoia, Wire Chair, Model 421, 1952. Knoll International advert showing the various cushion colours.

This was not Cold War culture; it was British national identity writ large as authentic craft.

At the Festival of Britain in 1951 – organized by the new Labour government to celebrate past British achievements and anticipate a promising future following the Second World War - named designer chairs made an impact, notably the Antelope chair and Springbok chair by Race. When visitors sat on these modern chairs, they were spirited into the brave new world of the Welfare State, and a science-fiction vision of future Britain. The skeletal metal chairs looked futuristic. Constructed from steel rod with balls for feet, the design echoed the official inspiration of molecular structure models. The seat was

Utility scheme display of Chiltern Rand at the Building Design Centre, 1942.

formed from moulded plywood in the case of the Antelope chair, a technique borrowed from wartime aeroplane construction. The seat of the Springbok chair was made from rows of springs. The chairs were used to furnish some of the outdoor terraces of the new Royal Festival Hall in London. Although the chairs were modern in construction, their form also echoed the British traditions of the Windsor chair. After the Festival the chairs were put into production by Race as garden or indoor seating. Another leading British designer, Robin Day, designed the seating for the Royal Festival Hall, and also chairs for the outside terraces. Day had already won MoMA's International Low-Cost Furniture Competition in 1948 with Clive Latimer, and this attracted the attention of the British furniture manufacturer S. Hille & Co. Hille were keen to mirror the success of the modern furniture trade in America, and selected Day as a suitable designer. He produced the Hillestak chairs in 1950; with their beech frames and moulded plywood seats they provided low-cost, mass seating for the new public spaces of post-war Britain – from schools to church halls and canteens. Day's designs for the Royal Festival Hall included the auditorium seating, chairs for the orchestra, and lounge and dining chairs. The dining chairs were supplied by Hille and featured a heavily upholstered seat, spindly metal legs and a moulded plywood back with wings that formed arm-rests. The chairs subsequently entered production with Hille, unlike Day's terrace chairs, with their slatted seating and backs, resting on a metal frame.

But the designers' identity in these instances was subsumed for the overall national interests, much like the Utility scheme. This continued with the promotion of the Contemporary Style by the Council of Industrial Design. Founded in 1944, this official quango was charged with improving the standard of British design to lift perceived levels of taste in Britain, and to stimulate international interest and exports of British furniture. The style, exemplified at the Festival of Britain by

designers such as Race, combined traditional British idioms with the fresh forms and new technologies being developed in America. Gordon Russell, who had been instrumental in the creation of the Utility Design Scheme, was the founding director of the Council of Industrial Design. In the 1953–4 *Daily Mail Ideal Home Book*, he advised 'On Buying Furniture' in which contemporary furniture was defined very much as the preserve of the professional designer, again reinforcing the link between the designer and the chair:

> I apply the word to furniture which has been evolved by thoughtful, trained designers who have studied the problems with care and who have worked for reputable manufacturers anxious to produce a job of which they can be proud. Such furniture will give lasting pleasure in use.[19]

Very influential in the creation of the Contemporary Style was Scandinavian furniture design. Perceived as more humane than the harsh metal of pure modernism, Scandinavian design used soft, warm woods, wickerwork and fabrics with more organic shapes. The chair's designer was also an important feature of the ascendency of Danish, Swedish and Finnish design. 'The Chair', designed by the Danish designer Hans Wegner, was a simple structure in high-quality, solid teak with a wickerwork seat. 'The Chair' was hand-crafted in Johannes Hansen's workshop, and the handcraft values of Scandinavian furniture were a crucial part of its appeal, when chair designers in the USA were aiming for more high-tech designs that could be mass-produced and looked cutting edge in terms of materials and construction.

The Danish company to go furthest down this route was Fritz Hansen. The architect Arne Jacobsen designed the Ant chair for Hansen in 1952 from simple beech plywood. The seat and back were

Ernest Race, Antelope chair, 1951, designed for the Festival of Britain. A skeletal frame looks forward to new technologies and back to the classic ladderback form.

moulded from one sheet of plywood and rested on three chromed, tubular steel legs, capped by black rubber. A copy of this chair was given modernist credibility by forming part of MoMA's design collection. A version with four legs was produced in 1955. Jacobsen also designed the more womb-like, Swan and Egg chairs, which cradled the sitter in a plastic shell with foam rubber upholstery. The chairs were designed by Jacobsen as part of his bigger project, the SAS Royal Hotel and Air Terminal in Copenhagen in 1958. The architect was responsible for designing the 20-storey modernist block and everything within, from the lighting fittings to the cutlery. The modernist block, and the dimly lit, functional interior was enlivened by the organic forms of the chairs. One architectural critic found that

> once inside these non-committal walls, the guest finds himself in quiet, dimly-lit interiors – the rooms are soundless and softly carpeted. The muted effect is by no means lifeless, however. The grain of woods and the figuring of marble stand out under the soft lights, and the upholstered chairs by Jacobsen . . . almost startle by the distinctiveness of their shapes.

The Egg chair remains popular today as a modern design classic. The *Telegraph Magazine* featured an article on it in May 2008, which emphasized the importance of buying the 'original':

> There are a great many copies on the market. If you want to make sure you are buying an authentic Fritz Hansen made Egg chair designed by Arne Jacobsen, then look for the following:
> Genuine Egg chairs always have a Fritz Hansen logo or sticker including the year of manufacture underneath the seat.
> For the past five years every Egg chair has also featured a serial number engraved underneath the foot, which will enable the chair to be tracked

if it is stolen. Owners can register their number on line.

For the past two years all Egg chairs have Fritz Hansen labels of origin sewn into the fabric or leather.

If you don't buy on line or in a private sale, then beware of bargains. The originals do not tend to lose their value (in fact sometimes they appreciate). So if the price seems too good to be true, then it almost certainly is.[20]

The chair manufacturer, Fritz Hansen, is certainly capitalizing on its ownership of the Egg design copyright. In 2008 the company released

Arne Jacobsen, Ant chair, 1952, designed for the chair manufacturer Fritz Hansen, seen here in production.

a limited edition of 999 anniversary Egg chairs in leather and suede for £7,500, all of which sold out. The standard model sold for £3,000 in the same year and also featured in its own room – Room 606 – at the revamped SAS Royal Hotel in Copenhagen, along with the original 1950s decor. Copies of the chair produced by companies such as Mojo Interiors cost £200 and are in the style of Arne Jacobsen, yet have a mini-biography and portrait on the website to authenticate the product, like a piece of fine art.

Arne Jacobsen, Egg chair, 1958, designed for Fritz Hansen. Chair among furniture in a room at the SAS Hotel, Copenhagen, also designed by Jacobsen.

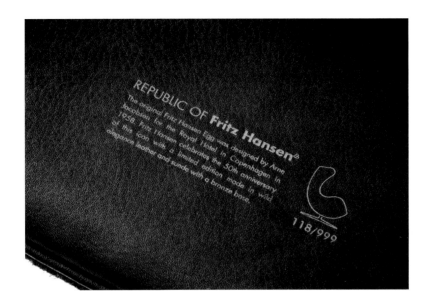

REPUBLIC OF *Fritz Hansen*®

The original Fritz Hansen Egg was designed by Arne Jacobsen for the Royal Hotel in Copenhagen in 1958. Fritz Hansen celebrating the 50th anniversary of this icon with a limited edition made in wild elegance leather and suede with a bronze base.

118/999

MoMA had not only been an important catalyst for promoting chairs as art, it was also an important inspiration for the founding of the Institute of Contemporary Arts (ICA) in London in 1946, and CIA/United States Information Service resources were pumped into the ICA during the 1950s. The chair was rarely exhibited in museums and galleries in London during the 1950s, but it found its way into the exhibition programme at the ICA. The display tactics differed from that of MoMA, in that it was an exploration of furniture design in relation to technology and fashion, rather than a litany of great designers. It is therefore not surprising that the exhibition 'Tomorrow's Furniture' of 1952 was curated by Independent Group member Toni del Renzio with the assistance of Freda Paolozzi (wife of the artist Eduardo Paolozzi, who was working at the ICA as a gallery assistant). The ceiling of the exhibition space was covered with a printed textile by Eduardo in typical messy, Brutalist style. Del Renzio was keen to

Fritz Hansen, stamp of authenticity on the bottom of the Egg chair.

point out the links with work by Sigfried Giedion and also contemporary Italian, Scandinavian and American design. The exhibition contained prototype furniture by British designers, including chairs by Clive Latimer, Ernest Race, James Stirling and Robin Day. But none of it was the classic, architect-designed chairs of the Modern Movement; it was more like a trade show or the Ideal Home exhibition in both its design and content.

The Independent Group, which met at the ICA from 1952 until 1955, was crucial to this challenge to cultural norms. The work of one member, Nigel Henderson, pushed back the boundaries in terms of the acceptability of photography as a vital instrument for the production of signs. The Independent Group ceased to meet in 1955, but in the following year made a significant contribution to the exhibition 'This is Tomorrow', held at the Whitechapel Art Gallery in London. The exhibition was designed by twelve groups which consisted, loosely, of an artist, an architect and a sculptor. Erstwhile Independent Group members, architects Alison and Peter Smithson, artist Eduardo Paolozzi and the photographer Nigel Henderson formed Group 2. The group was photographed sitting on Eames chairs, rather incongruously, in a London street. In fact, the location was the Smithsons' home at 46 Limerston Street, Chelsea, where, ironically, it meets Camera Place. The use of these design icons associated the architects and artists with their heroes, the Eameses, inviting them to share their PR photograph and to be an important part of their constructed public identity. It is important to bear in mind the significance of this group of people of American architecture and design, and of MoMA, mingled with an impressive knowledge of European modernism. As Alison and Peter Smithson observed in 1994:

Now chairs have always been the forward-runners of design change. They have for some mysterious reason the capacity for establishing a

E
PAOLOZZI

P
SMITHSON

A
SMITHSON

N
HENDERSON

new sense of style almost overnight. Rietveld established a whole new design mode with a chair. So did Mackintosh with his . . . In a sense both the machine-aesthetic and the Eames-aesthetic are art forms of ordinary life and ordinary objects seen with an eye that sees the ordinary as also magical . . . Eamses' chairs are the first chairs which can be put into any position in an empty room. They look as if they had alighted there . . . the chairs belong to the occupants, not to the building.[21]

The Independent Group was also aware of the latest innovations in Italian chair design from design magazines, as well as from a talk by Gillo Dorfles, editor of *Stile Industria*. Italian designers took the designer chair to a new level. Devastated by the effects of the Second World War, Italy benefitted from American investment in the postwar era as part of the Marshall Plan. This stimulated a renaissance in exclusive furniture design, clustered around the northern city of Milan. This was – and is – the cultural, industrial and economic capital of Italy, and it also accommodated international design fairs including the Milan

The Independent Group photographed on Eames chairs: double-page spread from *This is Tomorrow* catalogue, 1956.

Triennale, the Milan Furniture Fair and Eurodomus. The neighbouring area of Brianza was the location for many furniture manufacturing companies. The company Cassina modernized quickly after they had won a contract to supply furniture to ships, needing to establish a means of mass-producing design objects. They worked with the architect and editor of the influential Italian design magazine *Domus*, Gio Ponti, who designed the Superleggera chair for Cassina in 1956. Constructed from ash with a finely woven, twill cane seat, it combines the traditional, Italian form of the Chiavari fisherman's chair with the spiky forms of the 1950s. The chair was also available with a cellophane rush seat and entered the ubiquitous MoMA collection in that format as a donation from the manufacturer.

The early post-war years witnessed the ascendancy of the modern designer chair as a stand-alone object that could be used to represent national identities and the future aspirations of the West in an open-plan setting. This was further reinforced through a series of exhibitions that took place from 1970 onwards, which enhanced the significance of the designer chair and rationalized its development in terms of the modernist avant-garde.

It was the exhibition 'Modern Chairs, 1918–1970' held at the Whitechapel Art Gallery in London in 1970 that really provided the first thorough overview of the trajectory of architects' chairs in Britain. The exhibition consisted of 120 chairs, many of which were drawn from the V&A's own collection. In the exhibition catalogue, each chair has one page devoted to it, with a portrait of the designer, a photograph of the chair and chronological details of its inception and production. This is one of the first instances in London where a direct link is made between designer and chair, where the boundaries become blurred between creator and created. It also marks the point at which the modern furniture reproduction market began to take off, many manufacturers giving details for the entries. For example,

Publicity shot for Gio Ponti, Superleggera chair, Cassina I Contemporanei, 1956.

Knoll International reproduced Mies van der Rohe's Barcelona and Brno chairs, and Cassina produced copies of Le Corbusier's *Grand Confort* and the B306 chaise longue. This was still at the time when such objects were expensively reproduced under licence, and demand came from a small circle of cognoscenti. For example, Herman Miller sold 3,500 sets of the Eames Lounge chair and ottoman in 1969 in the USA (the highest figure for the 1960s). One of the purchasers of the Vitra Design Museum's European version was the design writer Reyner Banham, who admitted to having an Eames Lounge chair. In his incisive essay for the catalogue reprinted from his regular contributions to *New Society* on 20 April 1967, entitled 'The Chair as Art', he wrote that:

> I have a chair which, though designed by a famous name (Charles Eames), is also comfortable enough for me to sit in it for the whole evening. But the slope of the seat and its flexible mounting make it dangerous to stand on, and its shiny surface (which facilitates necessary fidgeting) guarantees that any cats, visiting babies, boxes of colour slides or current numbers of *Nova* that are placed on it will slide through the back onto the floor.[22]

Interestingly, Banham describes the new development of the chair as an art object:

> Almost every chair of consequence in our current environment has its designer's handwriting all over it; is signed as surely as a painting. Chairs are known by the maker's name (Parker-Knoll, for example) only in default of a known designer.[23]

The 'Modern Chairs 1918-70' exhibition reinforced what Reyner Banham in his *New Society* article, three years earlier, had so accurately observed.

The special link between modern designer and chair was again made in 1974 when *The Modern Chair: Classics in Production* was published by Studio Vista in London. The author, a New York-based Minimalist sculptor, Clement Meadmore, attested to this special link in his introduction:

Certain of these chairs are kept on the market by people who buy them for the name of their famous creator, or for the implication of design integrity they are thought to confer. I hope that perhaps a greater understanding of the chairs' real qualities may make for a less precious attitude to good design, and a less unquestioning acceptance of the status-symbol chair as a kind of stylistic name-dropping.[24]

Despite his best intentions, however, Meadmore follows the familiar chronological succession of modern chair designs and has a designer's name attached to each one.

Linda Brown and Deyan Sudjic curated an important exhibition at the ICA in 1988 that reinforced the chair as an art link by appropriating contemporary British design into the frame. 'The Modern Chair' consisted of 38 chairs, dating from William Morris's Sussex armchair of 1860 (lent by the William Morris Gallery) to Jasper Morrison's Thinking Man's chair of 1986. Like the Whitechapel Gallery show, many of the exhibits were modern reproductions, including Cassina copies of Mackintosh chairs and a Habitat copy of Breuer's Wassily chair, which irritated many contemporary critics, including Craig Allen in Crafts magazine. This reveals the deeply held belief that only authentic, limited editions of art or craft objects should be seen in the gallery space, the idea of the fake or knock-off is threatening to the world of high culture. The 'Marcel Breuer' show (1981) at MoMA and 'Mackintosh to Mollino' (1984) at the Barry Friedman Gallery, New York, also reinforced the chair as an art theme, which is still seen very much in evidence at the German-based Vitra Design Museum and the Design Museum in London.

Slightly less reverent was the RIBA exhibition 'Sit!' of 1982. This comprised 130 'of the best designed chairs of today',[25] which, unusually, visitors to the exhibition could sit on. This was largely because the chairs had been lent by the furniture distributors and so were modern facsimiles. But the show did explore the relationship between the body and the chair in ways in which the more purist 'chair as modern art' approach did not. In the introduction to the modest catalogue, Deyan Sudjic outlined a 'Survey of the 20th century chair' in which he did acknowledge, like Banham before him, that the chair was standing in for art:

> The Red-Blue chair has now taken on the trappings of a rarefied classic, produced like a limited edition work of art – a curious fate in view of the pains which Rietveld took to ensure it could be made by any jobbing carpenter.[26]

Since the 1980s, high-status furniture manufacturers and sellers have endeavoured to use a mixture of PR and copyright law to protect the exclusivity and premium prices of their products. Herman Miller, Knoll and Cassina have all attempted to stem the tide of cheap copies, since designer chairs are more freely available, as long as they are in the 'style' of the designer, rather than claiming to be the authentic object itself. The Internet and the heightened globalization of manufacture and distribution have made access to design classics simple.

For example, the American manufacturers Herman Miller took out an individual patent on the Eames Lounge chair and ottoman in 2003, followed by Knoll, which patented its Mies van der Rohe's Barcelona collection of chair, stool, couch and table with the US Patent and Trademark Office. This allowed Knoll to sue makers and sellers of cheap copies of Mies furniture, including the seizing of illegal imports. In Europe, Vitra owns the right to distribute Eames and Mies chairs. A confused potential buyer asked what the difference was between a Vitra Eames Lounge chair at €6,800 and a copy at €1,200. A Vitra spokeswoman advised him: 'It's a matter of emotion; if you want to own the real thing that is approved by the Eames foundation you buy that one. If you don't really care about the feeling, you buy the other replica.' The potential buyer mused: 'I am confused; is it really only the emotion/feeling that makes the 5600 Euro difference?'[27] Well, in a sense, yes. The authentic designer chair remains an important facet of contemporary consumer society, an investment and a status symbol. The cachet of the authentic displays cultural capital and privileged knowledge.

Nowadays any manufacturer anywhere in the world can mass-produce a designer chair, as long as it is in the style of the original designer. These signature objects are still promoted by means of the designer's biography and link to classic modernism. Despite high-end furniture manufacturers' taking out a copyright, such moves lack any real power. The consumer now has more control in this commodity culture. The makeover media have stimulated an almost constant process of restyling interiors, using the full gamut of historic styles, modernism being the most significant. Homemakers are free to mix Le Corbusier with Arne Jacobsen – be it the 'copy' or 'authentic original' – and with the issue of originality the degree of concern is down to the consumer.

It is interesting to contrast this designer chair as metaphor with the anonymous chair, the chair without a named designer, without the aura of authenticity. What anthropomorphic meanings can such chairs represent? Do they now reflect the power of the user, or the self, rather than the power of the designer over space? Looking at the famous 1990s British sitcom *The Royle Family*, which was set entirely in a living room, the answer is clearly yes. Chairs within the home reflect hierarchies of power between the inhabitants and also visitors. And modern designers may not even feature. The occupants may now mix and match their style, and the power is firmly with them in the commodity culture of postmodernity.

3 Luxury and Comfort

The idea of luxury and comfort is more a matter of aspiration and representation, an ideal, rather than a physical reality.[1] And ideas about what is comfortable and what is luxurious alter as social and cultural mores change. What was considered comfortable by a Victorian middle-class patriarch is different from what a teenager reckoned was cool in the 1960s. Comfort is also a psychological phenomenon just as much as a physical or cultural one. And some bodies at certain stages are never able to find comfort or luxury in a chair. The search I undertook for a comfortable chair when cancer had affected my partner's bones was fruitless. I bought two leather-upholstered, easy reclining chairs with matching footstools. His maximum stay in one of these was approximately an hour, depending on the morphine levels. He was also unable to go out for meals, sit in a pub or sit for long on a domestic chair; this essentially brought our social life to a halt – the ability to sit in a chair is central to Western sociability. We then bought two kneeling chairs. This, we hoped, would take the pressure off the vulnerable part of his body, and redistribute the weight to his knees. However, these too proved useless for him and he eventually took to lying in bed most of the day and night.

So the chair is part of the glue that holds Western culture together, one of the devices that amplifies social roles and perceptions of normative, physical abilities. It might be expected that physical comfort is the holy grail of any chair designer, chair maker or chair user, but the history of the chair demonstrates that it is psychological comfort, luxury and fashionability that have been far more important. Whilst the classic, modern chair was part of the ascendancy of the hero architect or designer, the creation of the luxurious and comfortable chair was more in the realm of the upholsterer, and later the interior decorator. Indeed, it is difficult not to see the two developments as diametrically opposed. The modernist architect relied upon metal, wood and leather to construct frameworks that elegantly held the sitter in space, in minimal surroundings, against stark backgrounds. Alternatively, the ideal of domestic comfort drew ideas from fashionable dress and textiles for the construction of the chair, with plump cushions and low seats, so that a relaxed posture was engendered. By the and the era of Pop design, chairs were designed to accommodate the relaxed culture of 'Swinging London', challenging the strict lines of the modernist chair.

Before the nineteenth century the chair was predominantly used as a ceremonial device, as a status symbol, as an object on which to perform the politeness of eighteenth-century society whilst drinking tea or playing cards, or reinforcing the status of the domestic patriarch. The idea of lounging in a comfortable chair was not a cultural consideration. Chairs were designed to hold the occupant in the correct and erect posture, ensuring that wigs did not slip and clothing did not become dishevelled. As John E. Crowley described the chair in the eighteenth century: 'Seating furniture provided a prop for the ordering of social status. The primary purpose of furniture was to express genteel taste.'[2] Easy chairs or upholstered armchairs did exist, but were used in the bedroom for invalids, and often doubled as a commode. It was only in Victorian times that the idea of comfort in terms of a satisfaction with your relationship with the physical reality of the world around you came into being, when the division between work and home became more delineated. The domestic sphere was the place for restorative relaxation, at least for the male inhabitant. The diary of Thomas Pumphrey, a grocer and leather seller from Newcastle upon Tyne, extolled the virtues of an easy chair at home:

> The way in which I have been relieved so ably from business care has enabled me to enjoy the quiet restfulness of a happy home; to enjoy the opportunity for leisure pursuits – especially reading in my cosy arm chair with my book always open on my reading stand.[3]

Dictionary definitions of *comfort* usually include mention of the easy chair, for example *The American Heritage Dictionary of the English Language* lists '5 The capacity to give physical ease and well-being: enjoying the comfort of my favourite chair' under *comfort*.[4] But comfort for the masses in the industrial world was initially provided for the patriarch, offering the opportunity to relax in the home after the daytime demands of work. Reading took place whilst sitting on special chairs, as did smoking. Smoking chairs were produced for and used by men in the nineteenth century, whilst the sewing chair, tea chair and tatting chair were created for women. The domestic space was the woman's workspace, and the relaxation space was for the man. Women were industrious and teetotal to the point of tea-total, while men drank and smoked.[5] As recently as 1962 Elizabeth Kendall stated in her middle-class domestic advice book *House into Home* that homemaking is 'the one creative job any woman can do – and do all her life. She can do it in her own time and her own way and give pleasure and comfort to herself and others.'[6] Chairs for Kendall were strictly gendered in the sitting room:

> Men and women usually like completely different kinds of chairs for a

start. A big chair with bulky arms makes me feel trapped. I prefer a small armless chair in which I can sew and knit. My husband, like most men, likes a roomy chair to slump and twist in and says he doesn't like cushions but asks where they are if they're removed. So it seems only sensible to buy different sorts of chairs for different people and circumstances.[7]

Comfort was clearly a gendered concept, and was applied to men rather than women until very recently. The wife's role was to create a comfortable home for her husband, and her needs were secondary. As part of the coal-mining culture of the north-east of England, my paternal grandmother would always stand in the kitchen, while my grandfather and his sons ate; she literally waited at table.

The technological reconfiguration of the home was enhanced by means of the technical innovations heralded in by the age of modernity. The coiled, steel spring was patented in 1828, and by the 1830s it was widely used in upholstered furniture. This meant that the chairs needed to be more thickly upholstered to disguise the springs and thus became more bulky. Deep buttoning and luxurious upholstery disguised the workings within.

The upholsterer or, in French, *tapissier*, grew in prominence in designing the interior and its furnishings from 1800 onwards. He was despised by modernist critics such as Sigfried Giedion:

The upholsterer (*tapissier*) is a man whose concern is with fabrics and their arrangement . . . In the nineteenth century, the upholsterer becomes identical with the decorator who, from the days of the Empire style on, debased the cabinetmaker's craft. As we have seen, his peculiar function began around 1800 with profuse curtains, crossdraped at the windows (*croisée*) and hanging on the walls. Later, under the Restoration, he also took possession of the furniture. At his hands chair and sofa became bulky pieces of upholstery.[8]

This view was shared by John Gloag: 'Loss of grace in design corresponded with the increasing attention given by upholsterers to providing comfort.'[9] Arch-modernist Giedion thought that 'furniture was being camouflaged as cushions',[10] and he celebrated the anonymous, patent-designed chair in his classic modernist text *Mechanization Takes Command* (1948). Situated in opposition to the upholsterer and interior decorator, Giedion presented an historical account of anonymous furniture, designed in the nineteenth century by the engineer to accommodate the body without heeding prevailing fashion. In a classic, modern approach, Giedion criticizes the upholstered and valorizes the practical. He eulogizes the surgical chair, which doubled as the dentist's chair and barber's chair in late nineteenth-century America. The mechanics were all visible, and the patient or client was held still in a semi-reclining position that could be adjusted. Giedion pours scorn on the European equivalents, which were entirely static: 'In Europe the lordship of ruling taste left the barber chair an unyielding thing, as stiff and static as the railroad seat, the lounge, or the sofa.'[11]

The burgeoning middle classes in their new, suburban homes in Britain craved the appearance of comfort and luxury in the domestic setting. Sealed away from the threats of the external world, the Victorian domestic interior was designed literally to cushion and shelter the

Geoffrey Holme, Editor of *The Studio*, illustrates two examples of 'Modernismus' for his book *Industrial Design and the Future* (1934), and notes: 'The enthusiasm for a style or for decoration, devoid of purpose or restraint, produces freaks which may be temporarily popular but soon become objects of contempt.'

household from the new, industrialized world. The look was luxurious, but the physical experience was not, at least for women. Wearing a tightly laced boned corset, as most respectable women did in the nineteenth century, made sitting or lounging comfortably impossible. Trying to sit while your back and waist are rigid is challenging, as I can attest. Attempting to get in and out of a modern car while wearing a boned and laced waist clincher is virtually impossible, since the middle part of your torso is held straight. It is easier to stand, since sitting down – even with an upright back – restricts breathing considerably because the diaphragm is restricted. So women would perch on chairs that were generously upholstered, rather than lounge like men, who were less fettered. Movement consisted of hinging from the hips, and the process was further constricted by the wide hooped crinoline of the 1860s and the bustle of the 1880s.

Whilst the woman in the Victorian domestic setting was padded and upholstered, the mechanics of the restrictive undergarments were secreted by textiles, fringes and ruffles. Similarly, Victorian furniture was covered, with the technology of hidden support. A prime example of this is the French *confortable*, which used interior springs (the form of which was that of the traditional armchairs), or the British easy chair. Both of these two types of chairs were completely upholstered, with cylindrical cushions for armrests and deep fringing disguising the supporting feet at the bottom. The chairs were heavy and bulky, but looked immensely comfortable. They were placed squarely on plush carpets and decorated with lace covering, and the setting was plush and luxurious.

Why were such chairs so problematic for modernist critics? The underlying reason may be critics' espousal of modernist values, whereby the structure of chairs, like buildings, should be revealed, light should be let in and there should be no dust-attracting textiles, secret nooks or crannies. This view of furniture history pervades the work of John Gloag and Nikolaus Pevsner. Gloag labels the eighteenth century as 'The Magnificent Century' in chapter Six of his book *A Social History of Furniture Design*.[12] Here, furniture was simple, well made and lacked mechanical interference or upholstery. It was also created by the gentleman cabinetmaker, as opposed to the dubious upholsterer. Pevsner, quintessential defender of modern architecture, discussed 'The Evolution of the Easy Chair' in 1942:

> That less inventive energy was now devoted to easy chairs goes with-out saying; for the very campaign, now no longer led by Morris, who had died in 1896, but by Voysey, Baillie Scott, Ashbee, George Walton, Charles Rennie Mackintosh and others, was directed against that Victorian stuffiness whose very symbol was for many people the heavily stuffed easy chair . . . No wonder that amongst the original designs for furniture . . . there is hardly a proper easy chair.[13]

In 1880 Emile Zola's novel and description of a high-class pros-titute, *Nana*, was published. It described her boudoir and the stifling atmosphere of Second Empire France:

> The rooms, too large for her, had never been completely furnished. The vulgar sumptuosity of gilded consoles and gilded chairs formed a crude contrast there in to the bric-a-brac of second-hand furniture shop mahogany round tables and zinc candelabra imitating Florentine bronze . . .
>
> The bedroom and dressing-room were the only two rooms to which a neighbouring upholsterer had really given his attention. A faint streak of light gleaming between the curtains, one could distinguish the violet ebony furniture, the blue and grey hangings and chair coverings. In the warm, drowsy atmosphere of this bedchamber Nana suddenly awoke . . .[14]

It was the feminine, hidden, sultry ambience created by the uphol-

Syrie Maugham, All White living room in her Chelsea home, 1929–30, photographed for *Vogue*.

sterer that so perturbed modernist, male critics. And this claustrophobic atmosphere was created by upholsterers, interior decorators and often orchestrated by women. Disturbingly for modernists, this was a force regarded as something closer to nature than culture. Jacob von Falke, vice-director of the Austrian Museum of Art and Industry, defined the position in 1879 in the popular book *Art in the House*: 'taste in woman may be said to be natural to her sex. She is the mistress of the house in which she orders like a queen.'[15] Moreover, the role of the upholsterer had been transformed into that of the interior decorator by the early twentieth century, a professional role pioneered and populated by women.

Generally acknowledged as the first professional interior decorator, Elsie de Wolfe designed the interior of New York's Colony Club

Art Deco style: chairs designed by French designer Pierre Patout for the liner *Ile de France*, 1926.

from 1905. She travelled to Britain and France to source antique furniture, since the vogue was for what the Americans called 'Old French' or Louis XIV–Louis XVI pieces or reproductions. The chairs were often reupholstered in more fashionable fabrics and painted white and gold. Elsie de Wolfe also refashioned the interior of the New York house of her long-term partner, Elisabeth Marbury. The role of the early interior decorators was to stylize existing interiors, generally to the client's requirements. In relation to the chair, decorators would usually work with the clients' existing collection, source antiques or reproductions. In the early years of the twentieth century modern designer chairs did not fall within the purview of the decorator. Later interior decorators in the US used American colonial chairs in their interiors. For example, Ruby Ross Wood designed Swan House, Atlanta, Georgia, in 1928 with checked curtains and indigenous wooden chairs.

In Britain, the role of interior decorator emerged soon after it had in America. One of the first was Syrie Maugham, who created the famous All White room in 1929–30, which included her signature pickled furniture – the Louis XV chair in the top left of the room has had its paint removed and then been 'distressed'; the modern upholstery was then added. Maugham's decoration of Wilsford Manor in Wiltshire, the country home of socialite the Hon. Stephen Tennant, featured a riot of satin and silk. Ruched curtains and cushion covers, chairs covered in satin from top to bottom, finished off with a deep frill fulfilled Giedion's Gloag's and Pevsner's worst nightmare, as did Tennant's playful design for a drum chair to blend in with the circus theme of his bedroom at Ashcombe, also in Wiltshire, which included a bed designed by Rex Whistler in the form of a carousel.

The ascendancy of the playful themes of the interior decorator, or *ensemblier*, was paralleled by the inception of Art Deco in France as the ultimate, luxury style. The style grew out of an attempt on behalf of the French authorities and designers to compete with German avant-garde design. The apogee of the style was the *Exposition des Arts Décoratifs et Industriels Modernes* held in Paris in 1925. The international exhibition consisted of temporary pavilions on both banks of the Seine, with the majority occupied by the French luxury trades. This included all the major department stores and manufacturers such as Sèvres. The exhibition was a celebration of Paris as the capital of glamour and fashion. This was the first time that electric lighting had been used to great effect in exhibition design, and Paris became the city of light. As Tag Gronberg observed:

> Along the Pont Alexandre III, forty boutiques showcased an impressive range of Parisian luxury industries, with the products of haute couture predominating. This was an urban thoroughfare comprised entirely of brilliantly lit shop windows in which the boutique defined not only la rue but also Paris itself.[16]

The chair represented this new luxurious consumption perfectly. The work of leading Parisian *ensemblier* Emile-Jacques Ruhlmann was exhibited in the Pavilion of a Rich Collector. Designed by the architect Pierre Partout, the sumptuous interior featured six plushly furnished rooms, designed by Partout and Ruhlmann. The chairs by Ruhlmann are of a different category from the designer and the reproduction chairs beloved of the decorator.

The chairs combine traditional French forms, usually from the Empire style of the late eighteenth and early nineteenth centuries, with glamorous overtones. Tapered, fluted legs and simple, elegant forms characterize Ruhlmann's work. Also, he employed exotic materials and the best craftworkers. One example from the collection of the V&A shows an armchair with stained pear-wood frame and gold satin upholstery. Another characteristic of Ruhlmann's furniture is

MEUBLES THONET

LE CONSORTIUM OCCUPE 12.000 OUVRIERS

LA FABRICATION JOURNALIÈRE : 15.000 PIÈCES

SIÈGE CENTRAL A BRNO (PALAIS THONET) RÉPUBLIQUE TCHÉCO-SLOVAQUE

SUCCURSALES FRANÇAISES

PARIS, 137, RUE DU MONT-CENIS

& 192, RUE DE GRENELLE

LYON, 8, COURS DE LA LIBERTÉ, MARSEILLE, 95, BOULEVARD NATIONAL, ET 12, QUAI RIVE NEUVE

LILLE, 52, RUE RACINE ET 9, RUE DE BOULOGNE ALGER, 19, RUE MAGENTA

SUCCURSALES ÉTRANGÈRES :

AMSTERDAM — BALE — BERLIN — BOSTON — BRNO — BRESLAU — BRUXELLES — BUCAREST — BUDAPEST — CHICAGO — COLOGNE
CONSTANTINOPLE — DANTZIG — DUSSELDORF — FRANCFORT — GRAZ — HAMBOURG — CRACOVIE — LE CAIRE — LONDRES — MADRID — MILAN
MUNICH — NAPLES — NEW-YORK — PRAGUE — ROME — TIMISOARA-TORENTO (CANADA) — VARSOVIE — VIENNE

the exquisitely capped feet in silver-plated brass. Other materials he used to create an ambience of luxury and exclusivity include lizard-skin, ivory, tortoiseshell, sharkskin and exotic hardwood. But this was not the highly defined status symbol of the French aristocracy or Napoleon; the chairs were used to exude luxury and exclusivity in exhibitions and in private apartments. Ruhlmann did undertake official commissions, including a salon for the Musée des Arts Africains et Océaniens in Paris, opened to mark the 1931 Colonial exhibition. Designed by the architects Albert Laprade and Léon Jaussely, the room featured four of Ruhlmann's 'Elephant' chairs, which were exaggerated easy chairs, covered in deep red leather, with the gigantic proportions picked out in cream piping. These were chairs designed for official lounging, to exercise colonial control in the official exhibition space. Even when Art Deco designers worked with the modernist chair form of the cantilever, they added luxurious upholstery.

The Parisian department store Au Bûcheron employed Michel Dufet to run its decorating atelier, Le Style. His design for the office of the mining firm Compagnie Asturienne des Mines featured chromed, cantilever chairs surprisingly upholstered in zebra skin, with thick padding on seat, back and arms. The Irish-born Art Deco designer Eileen Gray furnished a Parisian flat for the milliner Suzanne Talbot (Madame Mathieu-Lévy) in 1933. The flat was strewn with zebra and leopard skins, and included Gray's Bibendum chair. This was another example of cantilever structure; the two corpulent wedges that make the back and arms of the chair, and the heavy, upholstered foam of the seat, appear out of proportion, as if the chrome support were too feeble to support the Michelin man seat. The chair has now entered the classic chair Hall of Fame, and contemporary versions are distributed by the licence holders, London-based Aram, at more than 4,000 outlets, although the usual cheaper copies are widely available. The other Art Deco chair to inhabit the trendy

Thonet ad, as reproduced in the Guide Album of the Paris International Exposition, 1925.

milliner's flat was the Serpent or Dragon chair. An original Eileen Gray version in black sold for €21.9 million at the 2009 auction of Yves Saint-Laurent's art collection. This was a soft, moulded, easy chair with the arms made of a twirling serpent, an exotic and enveloping chair.

Like all high-end Art Deco furniture, the chairs were heavily upholstered. The opposite to Modern Movement chairs, the profile of Art Deco chairs was not geometrical but curvaceous. The sensuous curves of André Groult's bedroom chair for the 'Chambre de Madame' in the Pavillon de l'Ambassade Française was shell-like in shape, with gently tilting back and heavily upholstered arms and seating, covered in plush velvet. Indeed, the couturier and interior decorator Paul Poiret virtually dispensed with chairs altogether, just as his fashion designs for women

Andre Groult, *Chambre de Madame, Pavillon de l'Ambassade Française, Paris,* 1925.

had dispensed with the corset, both gestures for the sake of greater perceived comfort and luxury. Women could recline on the overstuffed velvet cushions on the floor of his display barge, *Amours*, at the 1925 Paris Exposition, in loose, Empire revival-style gowns, revealing the inspiration of oriental sources and the Ballets Russes.

The luxury and quality of Parisian Art Deco was popularized by the new mass media. This included classical Hollywood cinema and magazine advertising and editorial copy, including *The Studio* magazine in Britain. The plush seating of the glamorous 1930s cinemas was modelled on Art Deco, with welcoming upholstery on the velvet, tip-up seats. The same covering was used for the ubiquitous three-piece suite, popularized during the 1930s in Britain and the Western world with the growth of modern suburbia. Four million new homes were built in Britain between the wars, and most living rooms featured a three-piece suite as a mark of comfortable modernity. The modernist reforming organization, the Design and Industries Association, held an exhibition that consisted of two-room sets in 1953. Entitled 'Register Your Choice', there was an old look and a new look living room, one

Art Deco interior by Roger Bal, featured in the Guide Album of the Paris International Exposition, 1925.

furnished in a popular style, the other in contemporary style. *Picture Post* commented on the traditional three-piece suite:

> Sofas and Chairs. In the left-hand room they are definitely good and superbly comfortable. Padded and rounded, they invite you to sit, curl, lie. They are upholstered in uncut moquette, which will wear for ever; and drawn up before the fire, make a family fortress of the room.[17]

But how comfortable were the Art Deco chairs and moquette three-piece suites? Whilst modernist critics deplored their sumptuousness and decorative nature, criticism also came from the developing field of ergonomics, used to study scientifically the relationship between the body and the designed world in the name of efficiency. 'Ergo' derives from the Greek for 'work', and '-omics' to manage, and the study of the interface between the body and objects dates back to the Second World War, when the efficient design of air pilots' cockpits was studied, although the word was coined only in 1949. Therefore, the psychological benefits of comfort do not fall within the purview of ergonomics – rather, it is the physicality of the body that is the focus. Since chairs are mainly mass-produced, rather than custom-made, there are standards in place that specify the dimensions of the chair to ensure maximum efficiency of use. Like standardized dress sizes or shoe sizes, there is no such thing as the standard body. The Swedish chair researcher Bengt Åkerblom supported the standard seat height of 46 cm (18 in) from the floor in his seminal report 'Standing and Sitting Posture with Special Reference to the Construction of Chairs' of 1948. However, human bodies vary dramatically in height, and what might be perfect for the average adult male might be extraordinarily uncomfortable for the younger female or child. If a chair is too high, then the thighs will take on a weight-bearing function that will affect circulation; the ideal is to have both feet flat on the

RMS *Queen Mary*, first-class sitting room, 1936.

floor. Conversely, if the chair is too low, then the knees will be positioned higher than the hip joints, which locks them and also prevents the natural curve of the back from forming.

According to ergonomics, the optimum dimension for the depth and width of the seat itself should be at least 43 cm (17 in) square, to support a body sitting at the classic right-angle position. A longer seat may appear luxurious and comfortable, as in the case of a soft and capacious club chair, but to help the legs and feet to be positioned at the right angle and location in relation to the floor, cushions may be needed to support the lumbar region, and push the sitter further forward. As the Alexander Technique teacher and professor of architecture Galen Cranz has argued, the main problem with ergonomics is that it takes the traditional, upright sitting position as unproblematic, natural and given. However, even if the most comfortable upright chair

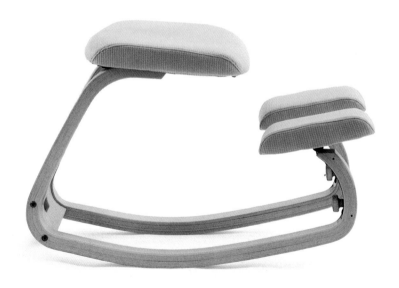

Balans chair. This ergonomic chair allows the sitter to rock back and forth, taking pressure off the lower spine. However, the kneeling position is unconventional and not for everyone.

is designed ergonomically, there is a problem in postural fixity – sitting in one position for any length of time is not good for the spine or the body as a whole: 'holding any posture for long periods of time is the ultimate problem; but holding the classic right-angle seated posture in particular has its own special stresses, which no amount of ergonomic tinkering can eliminate.'[18]

The kneeling chair solves the problem of static sitting, and I perched on one while writing this book. I found it much more comfortable than the conventional office chair, largely because you can move your body while still working, and the spine supports itself. Developed in Norway and first revealed at the Scandinavian Furniture Fair in 1979, the Balans (balance) chair holds the body in a position between sitting and standing. The design team of Hans Christian Menghoel, Svein Gusrud and Peter Opsvik dropped the conventional chair structure and replaced the four legs with rockers. You perch on a seat and kneel forwards on two pads. This creates an oblique angle between the thighs and spine of roughly 120 to 135 degrees. Therefore, the effort of sitting upright is shared equally between the muscles at the front and back of the spine, rather than just the backside. I can vouch for the comfort of these little chairs, although they look strange and feel weird to sit on at first. I used to experience extreme back pain when I sat writing on a conventional office chair but with the Balans chair I don't experience any pain at all, since the spine is placed in a position where the body is holding it upright, and you can flex the base of the spine by rocking backwards and forwards. The naturally upright posture also allows the body to breathe more easily, the lungs are not restricted and the pelvis is opened up. Manufactured by Variers, the chair is 51cm (20 in) high, 79 cm (31 in) long and 52 cm (20 in) in width. It is also lightweight, and can be lifted easily with one hand. It is available in beech or oak, taken from European sustainable sources. The padding is polyurethane foam and covering is available in more than 200 colourways. Cheaper copies are available that do not include the rockers, which negates the value of the chair, which lies in its ability to allow the body to move whilst perched. I can definitely vouch for their utility, although my osteopath argues that they are not a good idea for users with bad knees, and reaching from side to side, to switch the radio on, for example, or to get the paper from the printer, is bad for the spine, since the pelvis is in a fixed position. It is better to have a chair with wheels on. So the debate continues, and there is probably no such thing as the perfect office chair. I certainly do not choose to use the kneeling chair in order to relax. It is definitely a chair I would associate with work, sitting at a table writing this book. When I watch TV, socialize at home or read a book, I lie and loll on my new sofa. This is a modern T-shape design, with room for three people to sit conventionally, and an elongated part at the end, which allows me to put my feet up. This corner chaise design draws inspiration from the original chaise longue – an eighteenth-century French creation for the relaxation of the nobility. Like a day bed, the chaise longue has an identifiable place for the head and an elongated seat for the support of the legs and feet.

Such a posture for relaxation would have been unthinkable for a woman in Victorian times, but as the twentieth century progressed, slouching in the domestic arena became more acceptable as social behaviour became less formal. Designers such as Verner Panton and the Italian furniture firm of Zanotta reflected the more relaxed social mores with chairs with a lower centre of gravity. Fashionable living-room furniture sat lower on the carpeted floor; my trendy parents bought a leather sofa and matching chairs in leather in 1969. The sofa sat only a few inches from the floor, which we all loved, lounging whilst listening to the Beatles on the new hi-fi, but my poor grandmother, with her arthritic joints, found the seating arrangements too low. These changes can be traced back to chair design from the late

1950s onwards, when lifestyles and accepted postures became more relaxed, and so chairs were placed nearer to the floor or even replaced altogether by floor cushions.

Of course, this uses the type of conventional sitting used in Asia and Africa, which is gradually being eroded by Westernizing modernity. In the deeply ritualized society of Japan, sitting upright on the floor is still the most common form of physical posture for socializing and eating. Traditionally, food is served on a low table, with guests kneeling around it, and the tea ceremony uses the same arrangement. Guests are expected to kneel with both legs tucked under the body and the knees together, a posture called 'seiza'. Few Westerners are able to adopt this position for long, myself included, and increasingly many Japanese have become unused to this position for eating. In more casual settings, men normally sit cross-legged whilst women are expected to perch on the floor with both legs on one side, determined by the structure of the kimono. Sitting on the floor had predominated in Japan, but during the process of the country's modernization, which was accelerated during the Meiji era (1868–1912), there was an ever-increasing drive to adopt Western behaviour. Western-style chairs were produced in Japan for the export market; for example, the Osaka factory of the Yamanaka Company had offices in London and the USA. The Horyu-ji range produced by the company pandered to the Western taste for the Aesthetic Movement and *Japonisme*, featuring chairs with lotus leaves and phoenix shapes.

The Japanese government drove through a modernizing agenda, creating new industries and a consumer society. As part of this initiative, new magazines were founded aimed at women, including *Ladies' Pictorial* (launched in 1906) and *Ladies' Sphere* (1910). As part of this modernization of daily life, women were targeted as consumers and homemakers, and the creation of homes with Western-style chairs for eating was promoted.[19] For example, at the Daily Life Improvement

League house of 1922, constructed as part of a model home exhibition organized by the Architectural Institute of Japan, three rattan chairs surround a small table in the central living area. This arrangement was seen to reinforce the nuclear family group. However, such idealized model living had little effect on everyday Japanese living and sitting habits. It was not until the post-war era and the growth of public housing that chairs became more widely adopted in Japanese life.[20]

In the post-war era Japanese culture became more open to the Western seating position, just as the West became more relaxed in its use of the chair. Not only were chairs designed to be closer to the floor by the 1960s, but they also became more organic in form, enveloping the body, surrounding it protectively. Japanese designer Isamu Kenmochi's Rattan chair of 1960 is constructed from a

Verner Panton, Inflatable with Panton's first wife, Tove Kemp, c. 1960. The slender form of Tove in relaxed pose and casual outfit chimes perfectly with the innovative informality of the stool.

traditional Japanese material but in the modernist, organic form of a sphere. Inspired partly by Kenmochi's working relationship with the American–Japanese sculptor Isamu Noguchi, the chair is now for sale at the Noguchi Museum in London Island, USA, for $2,200 and has become a classic of modern design. The low position and rounded form relates to other modern designs of the time.

For example, Arne Jacobsen's Egg chair, dating from 1957–8, is soft and sculptural in form. Originally designed for the SAS Royal Hotel in Copenhagen (also by Jacobsen), it consists of a moulded fibreglass shell, upholstered in thin foam and covered in fabric. The curvaceous armchair rested on an aluminium base, which allowed the sitter to swivel around. Jacobsen was developing Saarinen's concept of the chair as a womb, which would enclose the sitter, perhaps with legs tucked up on the seat informally. This is in contrast to the formality of the modernist designer chair of the 1920s and '30s, and the severity of the SAS Hotel itself. Another Danish designer to work on more irreverent chair designs, to mirror a relaxation of social mores, was Verner Panton. During the 1950s he experimented with inflatable plastic to form a large stool for sitting on, which finally entered production in the 1960s. His wife, Tove Kemp, was seen perched on the stool in a cool, all-black beatnik outfit of plain polo neck and slim-fitting trousers with flat shoes, again, attesting to the informality of the age.

Panton's Peacock chair of 1960 consisted of an open, circular, metal frame with seven round cushions, placed like a peacock's tail. The chair is informal, close to the ground and designed for curling up on. Panton also designed the stackable chair in the same year, which is a free-form, fibreglass, S-shaped seat. Initially formed from moulded Baydur or hardened foam, then thermoplastic, it was the first chair to be made from a single material, in a single form and to be injection-moulded. With its sensuous curves, it featured in the groundbreaking women's magazine *Nova* for its controversial article 'How Yo Undress in Front of Your Man' in May 1971. Featured in bright red, the chair was photographed from the side in 24 stop shots, while the post-operative, transgender strip artist Amanda Lear removed dress, stockings, bra, shoes, knickers then hat. Panton then designed the 'Flying Chairs' for Herman Miller, which consisted of seating suspended from the ceiling. It made a huge impact at the 1964 Cologne Furniture Fair.

Panton really broke down the barriers of formal sitting in 1970 when he designed a psychedelic environment, with loosely formed seating as part of the interior walls at the Visiona II exhibition for Bayer at the Cologne Furniture Fair. This enabled visitors to the exhibition to strike a series of poses within the environment – sitting, lounging, lying down or positions in between. Panton was also the first designer to experiment with inflatable chairs, starting in 1960. However, it was the Blow chair, designed by Italians Carlo Scolari, Donato D'Urbino, Paolo Lomazzi and Gionatan de Pas in 1967, that gained the greatest popularity, and spawned thousands of copies. Manufactured by the Milanese-based firm Zanotta, it featured innovative technology with the seams that joined the PVC welded by radio frequency. Originally designed to float on swimming pools, the

Verner Panton's Panton (or 'S') chair used as a prop for *Nova* magazine photoshoot 'How To Undress in Front of Your Man', May 1971.

Scolari, D'Urbino, Lomazzi and de Pas, Blow chair, manufactured by Zanotta, Milan, 1967.

blow-up classics were soon emulated and made available in a range of colours, they populated many teenagers' bedrooms in the late 1960s. It was a perfect reflection of the hedonism and relaxed culture of the period, when throwaway furniture was celebrated. Blow-up chairs remain in production, and there is now even a specialist bondage version in black, with built-in arm and leg restraints – this particular version comes with a free mask. Disposable chairs for children in polyethylene-coated paperboard were also produced at this time. Designed by Peter Murdoch and sold as a flat pack in 1964, it came decorated with huge polka dots and could be disposed of after a few weeks of use.

The low, lounging style of the 1960s was further perpetrated by novelty chairs such as the Joe chair. Constructed from leather-covered moulded polyurethane to emulate the baseball glove of Joe DiMaggio, the body could be sprawled across the open palm and outstretched thumb and fingers. Even more relaxed was the Sacco chair, designed by Piero Gatti, Cesare Paolini and Franco Teodoro in 1968–9. Manufactured by Zanotta, it was a loose, sack shape filled with tiny polystyrene balls. Following in the wake of this design was the mass production of beanbags, oversized cushions in a variety of fabrics, filled with expanded polystyrene. They could be scattered

Blow-up Bondage chair, 2010. Inflatable fun beyond the swimming pool.

across the floor of any living space, to ensure relaxed lounging. Gaetano Pesce's Up polyurethane chairs were like circular sea urchins, compressed to 10 per cent of their actual size when packaged, and when this was removed, the chairs sprang into shape. Pesce also used the same technology to design the La Donna chair, with arms and quasi-breasts for a headrest; the chair was accompanied by a footstool in the form of a ball. Eero Aarnio's Pastil chair in moulded fibreglass was similar in organic form to the Up 1 and Up 2 chairs of Pesce, but in a less flexible material. Aarnio also designed the Globe chair in 1968 for Asko, which consisted of a large sphere, within which the sitter could curl up and hide from the outside world.

Tawaraya Conversation Pit, designed by Masanori Umeda, Memphis, and featuring the original Memphis collective, relaxing together in 1981.

The ultimate chair in comfort and luxury was provided by the 'Conversation Pit'. This was usually a carpeted seating area, strewn with cushions allowing relaxed sociability – drinking, smoking, TV viewing or even soft drug taking. The innovative Italian-based Memphis group of designers were photographed in Masonari Umeda's conversation pit, Tawaraya, based on the design of a boxing ring in 1981. The black-and-white striped wooden base holds 'Tatami' mats and silk cushions in a square ring, with ropes like those seen at a boxing match. The seating is finished with opaque spotlights at each corner. Such work was typical of the irreverent group of Milan-based designers. A proto-conversation pit also featured in films, including the Beatles' *Help!*, with the sunken sleeping area created for John Lennon in the band's home. There had been a revolution in sitting habits, at least amongst the younger generation, and social mores in general. As Paul Reilly, Director of the Design Council during the 1960s observed:

> The gap between the tastes of the few and the instincts of the many has been bridged to a surprising extent, even if not entirely in the manner anticipated – by which I mean that it is rather the instincts of the many (as expressed by the popular imagery of the Habitat/Conran/Carnaby/Chelsea/Beatles syndrome that have appealed to the few, rather than the preachings of the few to the many – but whichever way the traffic in ideas has flowed 'the friendly, human qualities of warmth, colour, pattern' have won through and Britain is now looked up to with some envy by her erstwhile mentors, such as the Swedes and Danes, as being a very lively spoke, if not the actual hub, in the wheel of change.[21]

However, such laid-back approaches to the idea of comfort were to be superseded in the 1980s and the era of postmodernism. As horror-fiction writer Stephen King observed of the late 1960s: 'I don't want to speak too disparagingly of my generation (actually I do, we

A Paris chair, designed by Martine Bedin, Memphis, 1986. Postmodernism in veneer and metal.

had a chance to change the world and opted for the Home Shopping Network instead'.[22]

Chair designers in the 1980s turned their attention to producing ironic re-creations and *mélanges* of the past. The Memphis leading designer and radical Ettore Sottsass used 1950s Formica designs to add a touch of trailer trash to his designer chairs. The Seggiolina da Pranzo chair of 1980 is a Formica-faced chair with chromed tubular metal legs, in a pastiche of post-war kitchen chairs, with chrome handles on either side of the chair back for an extra ironic twist. Architect Robert Venturi designed a set of moulded plywood chairs in 1984 that looked very similar in profile, but were differentiated by screen-printed decoration, representing different historic styles: swags and a classical column for Sheraton and a rising sun for Art Deco. Luxury and comfort re-emerged in the ironic revival of the 1930s plushly upholstered three-piece suite. In the first flat I rented in 1975 with my illustrator boyfriend, we were delighted to find a 1930s plushly upholstered three-piece suite in the living room. It matched the Victorian washstand that we had painted with purple gloss perfectly.

Another theme to attract the attention of chair designers in the 1980s was the office chair. With the economic and technical boom of this designer decade, office work – whether in the workplace or at home – was on the increase. The holy grail of the comfortable office chair has still not been realized, since the appearance and sitting posture of the kneeling chair still remains too outré, and there are also inherent problems with it. It is also impossible to design the perfect office chair, because every body is different, and everybody carries out different tasks in the office space. Contemporary office chairs offer great flexibility in terms of levers and handles to adjust them, but very few occupants touch them.

Mario Bellini and Dieter Thiel designed the Imago luxury office chair range for Vitra in 1984. The black leather, high-backed chair is constructed from an aluminium frame with polyurethane foam upholstery, resting on a chromed stand with five casters. The chair has arms to denote higher status, so would be destined for a senior manager's office. The computer operator chairs, for example, Bellini's and Thiel's Figura chair, tend to be upholstered in fabric, with lower backs, black rather than chrome support and less accommodating arms, if they have any at all.

In 1996, when I was appointed Dean of Faculty, I was furnished with an office supply catalogue and told that now I was a (reluctant) member of the senior management team, I could order an executive chair with tall back and padded arms, up to the value of £200. And I ordered it.

The most successful office chair of recent times is the Herman Miller Aeron chair. Made from 80 per cent recycled materials, it is covered in the breathable, membrane material Pellicle. Unusually for contemporary, mass-produced design, the chairs are built to last. In 1994 Herman Miller marked its fifteenth anniversary by offering a buy back scheme for the Aeron. Existing customers could get the chair refurbished or trade their old one in for a new one and new customers could buy reconditioned Aerons at a knock-down price. This office chair is also distinctive in that it recognizes that people's bodies come in different shapes and sizes, so the chair comes in small, medium and large, ensuring greater comfort for the office worker.

A chair never to be found in the traditional office, and one that does not denote status, is the rocking-chair. It originated as a type in the mid-eighteenth century, and consists of a wooden, Windsor-style chair with bowed rockers on the two left and two right legs. This enables the sitter to move backwards and forwards in a comforting motion. The motion of the sitter was capitalized upon in the early twentieth century with some outlandish inventions. The churn in the rocking-chair was patented in 1913 in the USA, and featured a butter churn beneath the seat, which swivelled as the chair rocked. Perhaps dubiously claimed to be an American invention,[23] the rocking-chair has certainly achieved revered status there. Generally accepted into the parlour as a respectable piece of furniture by the 1880s in North America, it is an essential component of even the most modest American home, although its acceptance into European homes came much later. The rocking-chair was the prime seat for use on the outside veranda at the front of the house. Writer James Agee and photographer Walker Evans conducted a survey of white tenant farmers in Alabama in the summer of 1936. Published as *Let Us Now Praise Famous Men* in 1939, the pair found that

> There are few enough chairs that they have to be moved around the house to where they are needed, but ordinarily there is a rocking chair on the porch and a straight chair in the rear of the hall next to the bedroom door. The rocking chair is of an inexpensive, 'rustic' make: sections of hickory sapling with other bark still on. On the hard and not quite even porch floor the rocking is stony and cobbled, with a little of the sound of an auto crossing a loose wooden bridge. Three of the straight chairs are strong, plain, not yet decrepit hickory bottom, which cost a dollar and a half new; there is also a kitchen type chair with a pierced design in the dark scalloped wood at the head, and the bottom broken through.[24]

Associated with motherhood and the elderly, in the chilling case of the film *Psycho* (1960) the rocking-chair is linked to both. This Alfred Hitchcock film closes in on the creepy Bates Motel. The heroine hides in the cellar and sees a figure from behind sitting in a rocking-chair, and taps it on the shoulder, but the figure is revealed to be the mummified corpse of the motel manager's mother. The familiarity of this cosiest of chair types is totally blown apart in one of the most shocking moments in the history of film. A more familiar use is in the *Beverly Hillbillies*, a

popular sitcom that ran on American TV from 1962 until 1971, in which Granny Clampett is frequently seen perched on her Shaker rocking-chair. The film *The Rocking Chair Rebellion* of 1979 featured the inmates of a nursing home having their lives challenged by teenagers. Further associations between the rocking-chair and reliability came with the Irish crooner Val Doonican on his 1970s British TV show. The designer couple the Eames reworked the classic lines of the rocking-chair with their 1950 design, which took their modern polyester seat on metal rods, placed incongruously on wooden rockers. Today the rocking-chair is marketed predominately for expectant and nursing mothers. The Country Hills Rocking Chair by an American company, KidKraft, is

Maclaren and other brand buggies at Park Slope, Brooklyn.

Lovely, Quaint And Country Styled!

Mom and Dad now have a comfortable place to relax and watch the kids play with this Country Hills Rocking Chair. With its sturdy construction combined with an elegant design of carved spindles and classic country style, this is a rocker that you'll enjoy for a lifetime! So rock your little one to sleep as you enjoy the comfort of this lovely chair that brings back old world charm.[25]

And once the baby has arrived and grown beyond using a pram, they need a pushchair. These were developed in the twentieth century as derivatives of the pram, which had been created by the royal garden designer William Kent in 1733. The smaller chair on wheels, which enabled the toddler to look ahead, away from the adult pushing it, was engineered in the twentieth century, but reached its lightweight familiar form of 'stroller' (in the US) and 'buggy' (in the UK) only when a retired aeronautical engineer, Owen Maclaren, developed it in 1965. Tired of hauling his granddaughter's heavy pram around during transatlantic travel, he created a more lightweight, fold-away, pushable chair for infants, constructed from tubular aluminium with a one-handed umbrella-style opening and shutting device. I used the same Maclaren pushchair for both my daughters, its attraction lying in the fashionable fabric and colour and its ability to lie the baby flat to form a quasi-pram, but without the bulk. Since the 1960s these have developed into large and complex constructions in a variety of colourways and fabrics, with double pushchairs designed for twins or children near each other's ages, to sit side by side, or one in front of the other.

Pushchairs liberated the child carer in the twentieth century, and enabled them to visit the shops or the local park more easily. Public transport could be more easily accessed and lifts negotiated, when previously those with young children were housebound unless they could rely on their extended family, or older children, for help. And with the rise in car ownership, pushchairs could be easily stored in the boot. Chairs designed for invalids date back much earlier, mainly for royal patrons. There is a sketch of Philip II of Spain in a chair with wheels at the end of each leg, dating from the mid-sixteenth century. Just like Louis XIV in the seventeenth century, and his special chair designed for him to be pushed around the grounds of Versailles, these royal wheelchairs relied on courtiers or servants to push them. The bath chair, invented by John Dawson, to enable the less able-bodied to be wheeled to the spa waters, consisted of a covered chair with wheels on the front, enabling the occupant to steer the chair. The bath chair was either pushed by a helper or pulled by a donkey or small horse. Wheelchairs developed their more familiar form in the Victorian era, with large back wheels that could be turned by the user, allowing more independence. Their use was enhanced in 1881 with the intro- duction of smaller rims within the large wheels, ensuring that the incumbent did not get muddy hands. Since that time, designers and manufacturers have produced wheelchairs using lighter and more robust materials, including wicker in a metal frame at the beginning of the twentieth century. Additional adjustability was also introduced, including the angle of the backrest and foot rests. With the advent of the car, transporting such objects was a problem, so more port- able chairs were mass-produced from the 1930s onwards by Everest and Jennings, starting in the US. The motorization of the wheelchair made them far more user friendly and guaranteed greater independ- ence for the less able-bodied. Such is the prejudice in Western society that occupants of wheelchairs struggle to be acknowledged when out and about. This has improved recently with more funky designs for wheelchairs and events such as the Paralympics, which display the achievements of the less able. Wheelchairs can now be individu- ally customized and have adopted the stylistic idioms of motorcycle

customization. The new design company of Nomad, founded in the UK by a wheelchair user, Mark Owen, has produced a minimal and stylish wheelchair that recently won the First Time Design Project Award from the European DME organization. Owen has argued that: 'Wheelchairs are now being considered as design items, not simply medical ones, and our branding is being seen as aspirational, which is unheard of in mobility circles. We really are very proud.'[26] Despite such eye-catching designs, if everyone else is walking or standing, then the wheelchair user is at an immediate disadvantage, and the able-bodied may not even make the effort to make eye contact. With pressure groups such as PHAB and the Disability Discrimination Act (DDA) of 1995 and 2005, the goal of inclusivity is nearer realization.

With our increasingly sedentary lifestyles and working practices, the well-being of our bodies – particularly our spines – is in decline. An estimated 4.9 million working days are lost per year in the UK due to back pain, and 80 per cent of the workforce will suffer back pain at some point in their working lives. Figures are similar for industry throughout the Western world. As part of our sedentary lifestyles, TV viewing is aided through the new wave of television chairs or sofas that recline in sections, in order that individuals may jettison a foot support. The teenage craze for electronic games has been enhanced with the introduction of game chairs, which are usually covered in black or faux leather, and include a sound system. The X-Rocker PRO gaming chair supplied by BoysStuff has 'wireless technology, stereo sound, ultra-powered subwoofer and vibration technology you can completely immerse yourself'.[27]

Ironically, the latest solution to back pain is the object that probably caused it in the first place: the chair. Massage chairs are now on the market that massage acupuncture points mechanically with a system of hydraulics within a heavily upholstered chair. Models are provided with music and adjustable footrest at a cost of

MRK1 wheelchair designed by Nomad design, 2009.

£1,500 or $2,000. For $4,500 you can have the massage movement in sync with MP3 music and have heated back or feet. So the positive benefits of Shiatsu massage or the work of the chiropractor can now be emulated with a plug-in electric chair. Sigfried Giedion would never have guessed that 'Mechanization Takes Command' would extend to such limits.

4 | Craft and Materials

How do materials inform the construction and style of a chair? What values are represented? There are categories of types in the craft history of the chair, for example, the Windsor chair, that have a perennial appeal for home and public use. Based on the use of traditional woods and other natural materials, anonymous craft objects act in stark juxtaposition to the experimentation of more recent craft objects, which use startling shapes and materials. With the recent blurring of boundaries between art, design, craft and architecture, chairs have provided a focus for designers to push back the boundaries of both form and materials. Chairs also provide a rich source of inspiration for the do-it-yourself enthusiast, from the ambitious construction of chairs to their decoration with loose covers, cushions and home sewing. The chair gives the designer-maker an opportunity to make a statement about beliefs, passions and aspirations for society. Indeed, many examples of handcrafted chairs make a strong statement about spiritual commitment, as in the case of the Quakers and Shakers, or political critiques of society, as in the case of the Arts and Crafts Movement and Droog Design.

The craft of chair making has a long history; the chair is an object invested with tradition and meaning. Before the full impact of modernity was felt, individual, one-off chairs were often constructed

from materials in plentiful supply locally. On a visit to Egypt in 2009, I took a peaceful boat ride in a traditional felucca down the Nile. Entering a small inlet, we moored and visited a small banana farm. On the farm was a simple chair, constructed from the palm leaves abundantly available on the farm. The chair was makeshift and rather precarious to sit on, but felt warm and welcoming. But it is difficult not to be lured by the romance of the authentic, which many craft products' promise. The chair has a reassuring, home-made feel with the lack of any trappings of modernity; the materials are home-grown and the object home-made without the mediation of marketing or retail outlets.

This kind of local craft tradition without the complexity of modern consumer culture was also evident in Britain as the Industrial Revolution

A craftworker restores a chair for the White House, Washington, DC.

began in the 1800s. A prime example is the Windsor chair, an icon of traditional craft. The chair has a solid seat, usually carved from a soft wood such as pine, into which the turned struts of the backrest, legs and the arms are inserted. The arms and back are often formed of steamed, bent wood. Originating in the locality of High Wycombe, Buckinghamshire, in the early eighteenth century, the chair was named after the largest and nearest established town, that of Windsor in Berkshire. High Wycombe was the centre for the creation of the Windsor chair, partly because there was a plentiful supply of beech trees in the surrounding Chiltern Hills. The town originally made chair parts, which were transported to London for assembly, but by the early nineteenth century High Wycombe was a national centre for chair production.

Windsor chairs have conventionally been associated with the values of craft, honesty and simplicity. This could partly be linked to the early methods of production. In the Chilterns were the 'bodgers', who often lived in makeshift accommodation in the woods or in High Wycombe's surrounding villages. The bodgers would buy groups of trees from estate owners at auction, which were then felled and crafted into chair

Palm-leaf chair, Egypt. The simplest, cheapest material is used to create a sturdy seat for idle moments on the farm.

stretchers and legs, either in the woods or in sheds near to their village accommodation. The parts were turned using a pole-lathe, which consisted of a length of sapling and a piece of rope. In a process that left no wastage, the 'bodgers' would use the wood shavings to feed a small fire to boil a kettle. The materials for the seats and other parts of the chairs were crafted by the pit-sawyers. They would dig a deep pit in the woods over which a wooden structure was built. The 'under dog' worked at the bottom of the pit, whilst the 'top dog' guided the saw above. Women were also employed in the production of chairs, usually crafting rush seating as piecework at home. The rate of production was such that in 1875, for example, 4,700 chairs were produced per day in the area's growing number of workshops. (So important was the Windsor chair to High Wycombe's identity that examples were used as the foundation for an archway of chairs, created for a visit by Prince Edward in 1880.) This hands-on, earthy approach to production continued well into the twentieth century,

Bodgers in the woods around High Wycombe. The workers create the component parts for chairs in situ.

Archway of chairs, High Wycombe, 1880. This precarious looking structure was erected to mark the visit of the Prince of Wales to Buckinghamshire's centre for chair production.

The symbolism of the Windsor chair as honest, affordable, vernacular furniture was established by the nineteenth century. Examples were to be found in taverns and kitchens but not in the pattern books that had been created for the prosperous middle classes, such as Thomas Chippendale's *The Gentleman and Cabinet-maker's Directory* (1754). Windsor chairs were produced by anonymous craft-workers, not named designers. They also symbolized a certain English-ness, as the American antiques expert Thomas H. Ormsbee declared in 1962: 'The Windsor chair was of English birth and breeding. During its long span it was as characteristic in a furniture way of English rural life as Cheshire cheese or Toby Philpot himself.'[1] An early example was imported by Patrick Gordon, the Governor of Pennsylvania, under the auspices of the Penn family in 1726. This Quaker state espoused the ethics of simplicity, and the Windsor chair was a fitting symbol for such beliefs. As Paragraph 41 of *Advices & Queries* states: 'Try to live simply. A simple lifestyle freely chosen is a source of strength. Do not be persuaded into buying what you do not need or cannot afford.'[2] For the Quakers, consumption was a visible sign of deeply held and controversial religious beliefs, and each individual was the source of spiritual wisdom and guidance. Whilst this spiritual sub-culture chose to use simple furniture, the items they did use then rose in status and importance:

> Asceticism attributes enormous power to the individual body: if God dwells in the heart of each person then each individual's subjectivity is uniquely a site of reverence. The implications of this conviction for social and cultural formations are immense and (paradoxically) gives rise to an intense preoccupation with the encultured body. How one organizes one's body in terms of voluntary actions, dress, speech and the appurtenances of daily life that act as supports to that body (furniture, place and tableware, textiles, vehicles for transport, buildings)

become a matter of intense significance. It is not merely a question of adopting a certain style of dress and mode of behaviour as a visible sign of group affiliation . . . [3]

So, perversely, the Quakers' 'less is more' approach led to a heightened sense for objects like the chair, and its greater significance. It was not a throwaway, decorative object, but a symbol of godliness and spirituality; thus it had an elevated status. When the translation of this belief system to North America took place in the eighteenth century, so the Quaker state of Pennsylvania and its capital, Philadelphia, became

A timeless Windsor chair, the mark of 'a simple lifestyle, freely chosen'.

the American equivalent of High Wycombe, the centre of Windsor chair production. Particular American variations were developed, including the 'writing Windsor' with a special small flat surface incorporated into the right arm. And a different range of native woods were employed, notably maple and hickory. The espousal of beliefs around simplicity, honesty and moral integrity were appropriated by eighteenth-century immigrants to America and incorporated into their national identity. The dichotomy identified by Philip French in his classic book, *Horizons West* (1969), also applies to the rustic simplicity of the American homestead, positioning the wilderness against civilization, Europe against America, female against male.

The Windsor chair remained popular in Britain, and in the post-war era in High Wycombe the Windsor chair motif was adopted by the furniture production firm of Ercol. The firm had been founded in 1920 and produced traditional furniture, including the Windsor chair, usually in beech. During the Second World War, the British government introduced the Utility Scheme and Lucien R. Ercolani, the founder of Ercol, was invited to design Model 4a of the Windsor chair for the scheme. From this foundation, Ercol went on to produce an entire range, displayed at 'Britain Can Make It' at the V&A in 1946 and at the Festival of Britain in 1951, using steam bending of wood in large quantities. Ercol also redesigned the Windsor classic in the form of the double Love Seat and Butterfly Seat, using locally sourced elm. Following the ravages of Dutch elm disease, however, the firm sourced elm from America from the 1980s onwards. Ercol continue to produce Windsor chairs, and Ercol's grandson, Edward Tadros, eventually directed an entire Windsor range from the company's factory at Princes Risborough north-west of High Wycombe. The chairs have a lasting appeal for the younger generations, as Tadros explained: 'They've rediscovered Ercol originals, such as the Butterfly chair, as well as our latest designs. Our furniture is still designed in Britain, and 85% of it is made here too.'[4] Ercol

continues to produce the popular Swan Windsor chair. The anonymous, craft tradition of regional furniture was therefore translated
into a named furniture range by the 1950s, and has gained a new
fashionability.

Another industrially produced, but nevertheless simplistic design
based on a distinctive, natural material was the range of chairs produced by the firm founded by Michael Thonet. He established the
Thonet company in Vienna in the mid-nineteenth century, with a
production centre and an early example of a retail outlet. Thonet was
innovative, both in terms of his mass production of stylish chairs
and technical breakthroughs. His main innovation was to bend solid
beech, using a similar method to that used to create the Windsor
chair, with steam. However, the process Thonet used was far more
mechanized, with a strict division of labour using a relatively unskilled
workforce. The most familiar of the Thonet models is the Model No.
14, or Café chair, with its beautifully arched back, flared legs and cane
or plywood seat. These affordable, lightweight, utilitarian chairs were
used to furnish cafés and bars, pubs and restaurants throughout
Europe and America. First produced in 1859, Thonet's café chair had
sold more than 50 million pieces before 1914, and still sells well.
Formed from six pieces of wood, ten screws and two nuts, it could
be made quickly by unskilled workers, who would steam the wood at
100°C (212°F) and then place the slats in cast-iron moulds for twenty
hours. The chairs could be stored and transported easily in parts and
would be assembled at the point of delivery.

This particular Thonet model held a particular, exotic appeal in
Britain and the USA, and was also used there to furnish domestic
interiors. Le Corbusier chose one of the Thonet Model No. 14s to furnish
his Pavillon de l'Esprit Nouveau at the Paris 1925 *Exposition des
Arts Décoratifs et Industriels Modernes*. Modernist designers admired
the simplicity of the chairs, and leading architects involved in the

Thonet chair, Model 14, or Café chair, first produced in 1859.

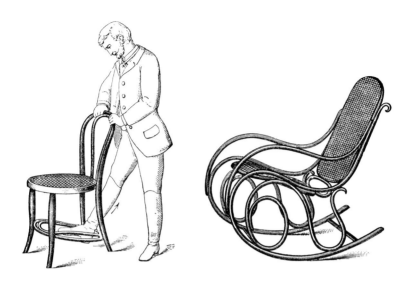

Viennese Secession in the early twentieth century designed both for Thonet and its rival, J. & J. Kohn. This included Adolf Loos, Koloman Moser, Otto Wagner and Josef Hoffmann. Thonet also produced rocking-chairs in the same solid beech, complemented by woven cane seats and back. These tended to be more decorative, with swirling Art Nouveau touches, and were particularly popular in the United States.

Modern Movement designers aspired to create chairs that were mass-produced, like those of Thonet, or at least looked as if they were. The craftworker, by contrast, usually works on the handmade, one-off or limited series chairs. This particular tradition dates back at least to the Arts and Crafts Movement of the mid-nineteenth century and the work of William Morris, Philip Webb and Dante Gabriel Rossetti. The chair types produced by the group were largely based on local, craft traditions with oak and wicker or upholstery. The working methods laid down by the Arts and Crafts Movement were then adopted by later designer–makers, including Ernest Gimson. He met William Morris in 1884 and, inspired by his example,

Two of many samples from the Thonet Brothers' catalogue, 1888, including the ingenious addition of a boot remover for the Victorian gent.

Ernest Gimson, beech and cane chair, *c.* 1895.

decided to learn the craft of furniture-making in a hands-on way. He therefore left the architectural practice of J. D. Sedding and became an apprentice to an established chair-maker, Philip Clissett. Gimson pursued his dream of living and working in a rural idyll, and relocated from London to the unspoiled Cotswolds along with brothers Sidney and Ernest Barnsley. They established a workshop there in the village of Pinbury and produced highly crafted chairs in solid beech and ash, based loosely on traditional designs. The chairs are beautifully made, with the form and construction harmonizing perfectly with the carefully chosen materials; they are a statement in wood. The workshop produced chairs that re-established a

Gustav Stickley, reclining chair, c. 1902.

lineage with pre-industrial British crafts. As modernist critic John Gloag observed: 'They did not pick up the threads of the English tradition where they had been severed in the 1830s. They ignored the Golden Age of Design, forgot everything that had happened between 1660 and 1830 and began where the mid-seventeenth-century English craftsman had left off, thus recapturing without antiquarian research or respectful imitation a true line of medieval development.'[5]

Shaker chair, c. 1900 – another mark of 'a simple lifestyle'.

Thus, Gimson and the Barnsleys worked hard at recreating a mythical ideal, based on a romantic dream of pre-industrial England, an England that could never be wholly recreated, even if they provided the chairs to sit on.

The handcraft aesthetic also resonated with the emerging national identity of North America in the late nineteenth and early twentieth centuries. The British Arts and Crafts Movement made an impact via magazines, such as *The International Studio* (the overseas version of *The Studio*) and *The Craftsman* founded by the American Arts and Crafts designer Gustav Stickley in 1901 following his prolonged visit to Europe. Stickley designed solid wooden furniture in so-called Craftsman style or Mission style, which expressed 'the fundamental sturdiness and directness of the American point of view'.[6] The stripped-down style also inspired the mass-producers of cheap furniture that had established themselves around the Grand Rapids area in Michigan. This style of furniture was also known as Mission furniture, echoing its beginnings in the Spanish missions in colonial California churches and furniture. It also became conflated with the Shaker style and the Amish style to denote morally superior overtones of the hand-built qualities of craft. Since the vast majority are mass-produced, however, the qualities are there by association rather than by actual production.

Shaker chairs, in particular, have become commodified and fetishized in the recent past as emblematic of a simpler and purer lifestyle. Much like the nostalgia of the British Arts and Crafts Movement, these elegant, ladder-backed chairs have little extraneous detail and simple rush, cane, canvas or woollen-tape seating. The Shaker religion was founded by Manchester-born Mother Ann Lee:

She was concerned with the eternal life of the soul, not with ephemeral things of the earth, such as chairs. Nevertheless, she believed that the outward appearance of things revealed the inner spirit. She cautioned her followers to shun the ultimately hollow pursuit of material goods.[7]

Chair-making was an important activity in the Shaker communities. Each had its own signature styles, signified by differently shaped finials on the top of the back post. The main growth in the Shaker communities took place between the 1820s and '40s when new dwelling houses were built, and chairs produced for the Believers to sit on. Chairs were often assigned particular rooms by a system of coding by numbers. The chairs are distinctive, in that they are made to slant slightly backwards, for a better seating position. Also, the slats at the back are narrower at the bottom and get larger towards the top. The chairs are not built for comfort, but for displaying religious conformity. Like the Quakers, the eschewal of the supposed evils of decoration and complication brings the user closer to God. One person, Thomas Merton, assigned the peculiar grace of the Shaker chair to the craftsman's belief that 'an angel might come and sit on it'.[8] The ladder-back feature is important, since it meant that the chairs could all be suspended from specially made rows of knobs high on the wall, clearing the floor space for Shaker services, which take place standing. Contemporary commentators found the Shaker style overly simplistic at a time when plush upholstery was becoming fashionable. Charles Dickens disliked the 'stiff high-backed chairs' and thought that Shaker living spaces resembled factories or even barns.[9] Hence, the simple Windsor chair and its ladder-back derivative became a symbol for radical Christianity and the ideology of the American West.

Simple craft ethics were also employed by many professional American architects. For example, beautifully crafted furniture by the architectural practice of Greene & Greene was produced in the early twentieth century to furnish spacious homes the pair designed for the wealthy families of the Blackers, Gambles, Pratts and Maybecks.

The living room at the David B. Gamble House in Pasadena, California, of 1908, for example, features handcrafted oak rocking-chairs
with clearly articulated joints, echoing the construction of the interior itself. Frank Lloyd Wright also designed simple furniture in oak
to reflect the honesty and simplicity of the construction of houses
he designed for wealthy clients such as Francis W. Little and Isabel
Roberts in the early twentieth century. Even the armchairs for the
Francis W. Little house were constructed from a visible oak framework, more traditional comfort supplied by an upholstered, removable
central cushion.

Whilst there is an important strand of handcrafted chair production that embraces the higher moral ground, there is another aspect
that uses craft and material in a far more decadent manner. The
Art Nouveau erotica of the Parisian photographer François-Rupert
Carabin is centred on a carved wood model of a bound, naked woman.
The chair is of a simple X-frame construction, but with surprising
elements. The arms are made of slinky cats and the legs of the woman
are cruelly trapped behind the back strut connecting the two legs of
the chairs. She is hanging onto the back of the chair by ties, linking
her fingers to the cushion placed for the head of the sitter – who
sits with his back to her, ignoring her suffering. Her eyes are closed,
perhaps waiting for the next whiplash. The hardness of the mahogany
is ironically used to represent the softness of the female flesh.

Art Nouveau decadence is also in evidence in chairs designed by
Carlo Bugatti for the Turin International exhibition of 1902. The sinuous, snakelike shape of the Cobra chair is constructed from wood
and covered in pale vellum with a decorated copper insert. It was
displayed in the Snail Room. The vellum was hand-painted, leaving
traces of the artist on the surface of the chairs. Such one-off, idiosyn-
cratic decorating of chairs was also enjoyed by the short-lived Omega
Workshops. Founded in London by the modernist art critic Roger Fry

in 1913, the painters Duncan Grant and Vanessa Bell took delight in painting poorly made furniture, particularly chests and tables, with Post-Impressionist colours and forms. A distinctive dining-room chair was designed by Fry in 1913 and produced by the British craft firm of Dryad Ltd. It was made from painted wood, red in imitation of lacquer, with a caned seat and back. A set of the chairs was used at the Omega Workshops' pinnacle of achievement, the Charleston Farmhouse in Sussex. The Bloomsbury Group rented the property from October 1916 onwards, and Grant and Bell remained there for the rest of their lives, Grant dying in 1978. The Omega Workshops also produced chairs decorated with needlepoint embroidery to designs by Roger Fry. The handmade quality of the Omega Workshops designs is a crucial feature. Textiles were also produced by the group and used for soft

The living room at Greene & Greene's David B. Gamble House, 1908.

furnishings, again, in strong colours and bold patterns. However, the Bloomsbury set were just as likely to use traditional English easy chairs upholstered in chintz with contrasting throws and cushion covers in their rather English, eccentric way. The personal touch of the makers here betrayed their enthusiasm for French avant-garde high culture, mingled with the decorative and the handmade.

It was not only professional artists and designers or religious communities who explored the creative potential of the handmade. As the home became separated from work during the eighteenth and nineteenth centuries, so craft became promoted and mediated as a worthwhile occupation for the respectable woman at home. The domestic ideal of the wife, mother and defender of moral rectitude had its roots in this period, and women were expected to manage the serv-

Duncan Grant's studio at Charleston, decorated in the 1930s by Grant and Vanessa Bell.

ants and the household and also take part in worthwhile pursuits. As late as 1925 the popular magazine *Modern Woman* declared that the 'real home' was 'a shrine of the most sacred things of life, love, birth, death, struggle, self-conquest'.[10] Worthwhile pursuits for women in the home included embroidery, crochet and knitting – all of which could be used to produce personalized textiles to decorate their domestic surroundings. Chairs in their own right were rarely home-crafted from scratch; reupholstering chairs or making loose covers was more common, but items to decorate them in the domestic setting were a frequent addition. At an interesting point between consumption and production, the maker becomes the user. The craft object represents the ideology of the homemaker and family. And these homemaking skills also involved the chair, whether in decoration or even recovering, as the *Young Ladies Treasure Book* of 1881–2 advised:

> Girls who are clever with their fingers can do very much towards making the home beautiful, not only by needlework, painting and drawing, and the various kinds of fancy work, but by the practice of amateur upholstery.[11]

By the inter-war years such personal touches were advocated by women's magazines as signs of modernizing the home: 'although men don't like fripperies and modern rooms scorn odd bits and pieces, both will accept joyfully this distinguished chair back in crisp crochet'.[12] The virtues of handcrafts at home were also promoted by the National Federation of Women's Institutes (NFWI) established in 1915, local authority evening classes and the Home Arts and Industries Association, founded in 1884 on the values and beliefs of Morris and the Arts and Crafts Movement. As Pat Kirkham has demonstrated: 'The boom – it almost amounted to a craze – for handicrafts led to a great demand for materials, tools, instruction manuals and demonstrators.'[13] The materials were supplied and promoted through instruction manuals by the manufacturer Dryad. Embroidery threads, needles and canvases were all made by Dryad to a high standard since the owner, Harry Peach, was a keen supporter of the Arts and Crafts architect and promoter W. R. Lethaby. One of Dryad's instructional publications by Dorothy Hart even covered the specialist skill of upholstery. The handicrafts boom of the 1920s and '30s in Britain continued in the post-war years. I remember my maternal grandmother, a stalwart member of the Women's Institute, making a footstool from empty Lyle's Golden Syrup tins, covered in upholstery with decorative piping. My paternal grandmother was an avid knitter and my mother a skilled home dressmaker. These feminine handicrafts were augmented by a Do-It-Yourself boom in the post-war years. Originating in the US, the commodification of tools, materials and techniques for extensive work around the home by the amateur couple had an impact during the 1950s, when official ideology emphasized the virtues of the home. The movement was supported and stimulated by the media, including colour magazines such as *Practical Householder* and *Do-It-Yourself* (the latter launched in Britain in 1957), and various television programmes. In the USA *Popular Mechanics* and *Family Handyman* supported the DIY industry. The magazines featured ambitious projects, including building a beach hut or your own three-piece suite from scratch. In the twenty-first century the cost of furniture for the home has fallen dramatically, since construction is often outsourced to Asia. Craft skills remain useful, particularly for the self-assembly of chairs from retailers such as the Swedish IKEA chain, which are purchased in flat packs for construction at home, a trend with consumers in North America and Europe. This drives down the price of the furniture because the price of air transport is not included, but the home assembly can require specialist skills and power tools. Most goods are produced in China. The rudimentary quality of

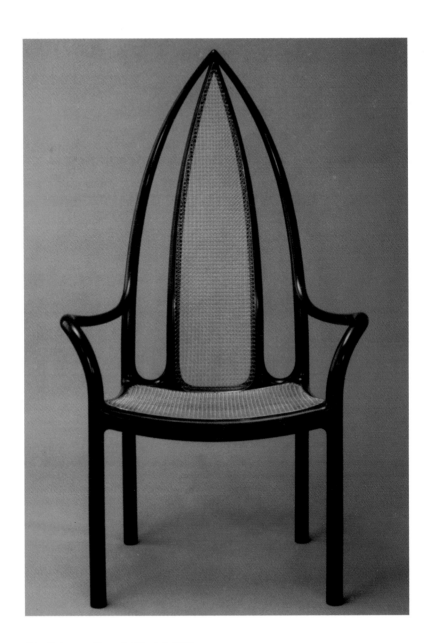

John Makepeace, Ebony Gothic chair, 1978.

Wendell Castle, Chair with Sports Coat, 1978. The coat and chair are skilfully carved from the same wood in this tremendous example of 3D *trompe-l'œil*.

much simple, craft furniture makes emulating it particularly appealing and simple, and today plans for Mission, Shaker and Amish chairs are sold over the Internet for home construction, particularly in the USA. However, websites that include details of how to build your own electric chair at home seem slightly ill judged.[14] But the prospect of crafting a chair at home remains appealing, as is the simple repair of chairs. As American furniture experts Beecher and Stowe advise:

> if you have in the house any broken down arm chair . . . draw it out
> – drive a nail here and there to hold it firm – stuff and pad, and stitch
> the padding through with a long upholsterer's needle, and cover it with
> chintz like your other furniture. Presto – you create an easy chair.[15]

Whilst amateur craftwork has a long history, professional craftwork emerged during the 1970s in Britain as a professional, creative practice in its own right, supported by the establishment of the Crafts Advisory Committee in 1971. The handmade was now recognized as being separate from the industrial emphasis of the Design Council in Britain. From the beginning, the Committee and the British Crafts Centre encouraged the elevation of craft to the level of fine art, rather than sustain the traditional handcraft skills. For example, John Makepeace, a founder member (1977) of his school for apprentices at Parnham House in Dorset, south-west England, combined craft, design and education. His work uses fine materials and high levels of craft skill to produce exquisite pieces. His Mitre chair of 1978 is finely handmade from an ebony frame complete with Gothic pointed-arch back combined with a woven nickel silver seat and back. Makepeace's fascination with wood is even more apparent in his Burr Myrtle thrones, which are solid pieces of sprawling wood with a seating compartment cut into the trunk. Another designer to found his own design school is the American Wendell Castle. He pushes the boundaries of what can be done with wood, and his Chair with Sports Coat from 1978 consists of a standard dining chair in solid maple, complete with a jacket hung on the top, carved out of the same piece of wood. His even more experimental laminated rocking-chair consists of a support shaped like a dolphin's tail in black, in which different shapes can be fitted to create a rocking-chair or turned the other way to make a cosy alcove.

The most prevalent trend in chair design in the 1980s in Britain was not pieces handcrafted only from wood, but from any material. The impact of Punk culture, with its cut-and-paste mentality and messy, dirty aesthetic affected chair design. The most prominent designer to use this bricolage approach was Ron Arad, who explored the use of recycled materials starting with seats taken from scrapped cars and remodelled into Rover chairs in 1982. They were displayed in the shambolic setting of his London shop, One-Off Ltd, which looked as if a bomb had hit it. The title chosen for his shop encapsulates a new attitude to chair design and production. Modernist designers always had the ideal of their work being mass-produced; they idolized the mechanised process, even if this ideal was not a reality. With the work of Arad the notion of the handmade aesthetic – but not in a craft sense – began to emerge. His chairs are not the perfectly carved wood of John Makepeace, nor do they contain the anonymous moral message of the Shakers; instead, they are almost like sculptures. Arad's work developed as an increasingly abstract exploration of the form and the materials of the chair. As Gareth Williams, Senior Tutor in Design Products at the Royal College of Art and former Curator of Furniture at the V&A, commented:

By focussing on what is new, Ron Arad has created a body of work at the intersection of art and design . . . Not content to be either a marginalized designer–maker, or a jobbing product designer working to a company brief, Arad has drawn from both craft and industry to create a unique space where he can create furniture and objects that initially exist to answer exploration of materials, techniques and symbolism.[16]

Arad continued to make design–art chairs, working increasingly in metal and other materials with signatures in limited editions of between five and twenty. In the 1980s chairs by designer–artists acquired titles to emulate the conventions of fine art categorization. Arad produced short runs of crucial designs, such as the Big Easy, an exaggerated armchair initially in metal with his own welds and hammer marks, in 1989. It was then professionally produced by One-Off Ltd in 1990 in shiny stainless steel for the collectors' market. In the same year the high-end furniture manufacturers Moroso produced the model in foam and upholstery. Arad then produced the shape in polyester, which he painted in bright, messy scrawls and called the New Orleans. It has been produced in carbon fibre and rotation-moulded polyethylene as well. Other chairs, such as the Big Heavy of 1989, aspired to be works of art. Arad made the rocking-chair from patinated mild steel, welded and finished by the designer–maker, using his self-taught skills. The At Your Own Risk chair of 1991 was made from mirror-polished stainless steel. At an opening at the private Carpenters Workshop Gallery in Mayfair, London, the piece was displayed alongside the the Big Heavy, After Spring, Before Summer and Loop Loop chairs in an ensemble of elegantly shaped metal. The gallery assistant carefully polished At Your Own Risk, which only barely resembles a chair, the title referring to the act of sitting on such a smooth, slippery rocking-chair. The two pieces, After Spring and Before Summer, from 1992 are huge loops of bronze, hard-edged and risky, like playground rides. Arad now enjoys the status of a celebrity designer and was the subject of a retrospective, *No Discipline*, at the Centre Pompidou in Paris in 2009. His work has also entered the collections of many major museums, including that of the V&A and those of private collectors.

As Gareth Williams has argued, Arad is part of an 'egosystem'[17] of star artist–designers who rose to prominence during the designer decade of the 1980s. Almost emulating the fame and success of the YBAs (Young British Artists) like Damien Hirst and Tracey Emin, the artist–designers work with specialist manufacturers, producing limited-edition objects of collectable value. The British furniture designer Peter Christian, reflecting on the decade, mused: 'The UK, with its reputation for eccentricity, produced its own crop for imported chair sculptors including Ron Arad, Danny Lane and André Dubreuil.'[18] Speaking about his own Rib chair on the eve of leaving for the Milan Furniture Fair, Christian protested: 'Although some of our chairs are in art galleries, we don't want to get into that kind

Ron Arad, Rover chair, 1982. The scrap-yard aesthetic of punk design.

of self indulgent area that is halfway between bad art and bad design.'[19] However, Christian's more down-to-earth approach did not find fashionable favour in the 1980s. The designer–artist creates an identity, even a personal brand, that can be bought into at a premium price. Another of the constellation of designer stars who explore the limits of materials and chair forms is Marc Newson. His celebrity status was confirmed in the 1980s when his Lockheed Lounge of 1986 featured in both a Madonna promotional video for *Rain* and Philippe Starck's boutique Paramount Hotel. Its sculptural form is created from a core of fibreglass-reinforced polyester, covered in riveted sheets of aluminium. Newson used more than 2,000 rivets in a decorative, expensive design. His sculptural Felt chairs were made from a fibreglass-reinforced polyester and an anodized aluminium frame with a bright, textile covering. The anthropomorphic shape is reminiscent of the smooth, organic forms and Pop Art palette of Olivier Mourgue, particularly his designs for the set of *2001: A Space Odyssey* (1968).

The leading exponent of the 'egosystem' is the French celebrity designer Philippe Starck, who has specialized in aspects of modern chair design. Unlike other artist–designers, Starck eschews unusual materials for plastic. He is so enamoured with the material that he has dedicated a poem to it:

I dream weird dreams
I dream of chairs
Rather than weep
I have made them my trade
While on a Paris-Tokyo flight
– too long – I dreamt of a small
solid chair,
so serviceable and considerate,

she wants to be plastic
and not kill trees.[20]

Starck designed the Toy chair in 1999, which was mass-produced by Driade Atlantide in polypropylene, and La Marie chair in 1998, produced by Kartell in Italy. Perhaps his most striking, and most emulated, design is for the Louis Ghost chair of 2002, again produced by Kartell. The clear plastic is deceiving, and makes the classic furniture profile look as if it is made of glass. Accessible and fun, 100,000 Louis Ghost chairs had been produced by 2005. Starck has argued that plastic is the most sustainable material to use for mass chair production, but he has also designed more up market, modernist chairs. The drum-shaped Costes chair with its distinctive three legs – designed for the Costes Café in Paris in 1982 – was made from an enamelled tubular steel frame, with a bent mahogany-faced plywood back and a leather-covered foam seat. The Ed Archer chair of 1987, constructed from a tubular steel frame with leather upholstery has only one, aluminium leg at the back – the front is supported by the leather-covered frame. Less sleek and reverential is Starck's jokey 'This is not a wheelbarrow' (*Ceci n'est pas une brouette*) of 1995. Manufactured by XO, is a conventional wheelbarrow constructed from ash has an upholstered seat and back grafted onto the top in a strange juxtaposition of ordinary objects. The inspiration partly came from the wheelbarrow chair of 1937 by the Surrealist artist Oscar Dominguez, and it retails for more than £3,000. The smoothness of the Louis XVI cream satin contrasts starkly with the paleness of the bare wood, not the gilded wood usually seen framing this type of upholstery fabric.

While Starck used clear plastic to emulate glass, another signature designer, Danny Lane, has used actual glass for his chair designs. Glass is a surprising and edgy material to use for the construction of a chair, but Lane has explored the limits of this particular material

in his one-off chair designs. Objects created by Lane from bits of sheet glass, stacked to create legs and backs, include Solomon's chair from 1988. He also made the Etruscan chair from two pieces of glass and connected forged, mild steel curved rods. The two slabs of glass have rough, jagged edges that have been polished, but they still look threatening and dangerous. A much softer, romantic use of clear acrylic resin can be seen in Shiro Kuramata's Miss Blanche chair of 1989. Red paper flowers with green stems were cast into the transparent material to form the chair, supported on red, tubular, aluminium legs. 'Miss Blanche' refers to the tragic heroine of the Tennessee Williams play *A Streetcar Named Desire*, and the chair represents the slightly faded, camp charms of this southern belle.

The same Japanese architect works effectively in metal, as is demonstrated with How High the Moon, a traditional armchair shape constructed from perforated zinc and steel mesh. Originally designed in 1986, it was reissued by the Swiss-based, high-end furniture manufacturer Vitra in 1987 as part of its highly selective Vitra Edition series. The stereotypical contours of a comfortable armchair have

Philippe Starck, 'Ceci n'est pas une brouette' (This is not a wheelbarrow), 1995.

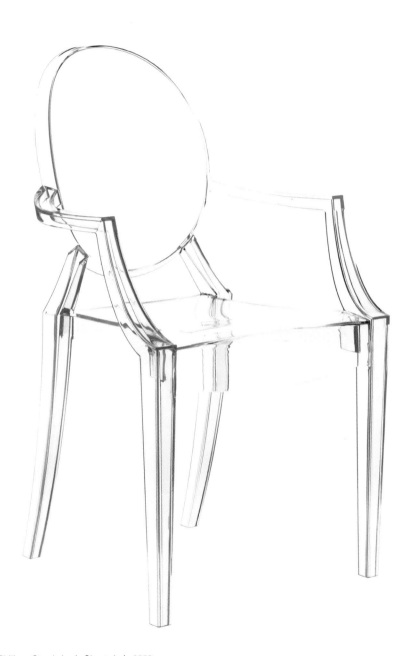

Philippe Starck, Louis Ghost chair, 2002.

been taken and reinterpreted in perforated metal, which challenges our expectations about comfort and function. Chairs like this are there to make a statement about design forms, to push back barriers and challenge expectations with a studied seriousness.

Other members of the 'egosystem' to emerge in the 1980s include Jasper Morrison. Less of an artist–designer, and more of a mainstream, modernist designer, Morrison first made an impact with his Thinking Man's chair when it was exhibited by Zeev Aram in his London showroom in 1986. Constructed from tubular and sheet steel that was then painted, the chair was afterwards taken up for manufacture by Cappellini in Italy. Aram owns the rights to Eileen Gray's furniture, and worked with her in the 1970s to revive her designs for manufacture. Morrison's designs are deliberately sparse and almost diagrammatic in their linearity. His 1988 installation for Vitra, entitled *Some New Items for the Home* in Berlin, consisted of a stage set with simple, wooden furniture placed carefully within it. His plywood chair from the installation consists of nine pieces of wood, simply glued and screwed together and left unpainted. The chair was later produced by Vitra. His most famous chair design is that of Air, dating from 1999. He collaborated with Magis, an Italian manufacturer, to mass-produce this plastic furniture. Using technology taken from car manufacturing, the design was prototyped using CAD (Computer Aided Design). It is formed from one piece of gas-injected polypropylene with chambers of air, which explains the name of the piece. Because of the use of sophisticated technology, each chair takes only four minutes to make, and more than 350,000 had been produced by 2006. The chairs are lightweight and fun, easy to sit on and add a touch of design class to their surroundings.

This kind of CAD and rapid prototyping has significantly altered the process of the design and production of chairs. The handcrafted, unique object still continues to be produced, though, for example, the Mid-Afternoon chair by the Japanese artist Yayoi Kusama. This consists of a traditional rocking-chair covered in a multitude of phallic shapes or dildoes, interspersed with roses and sprayed gold. Such extravagances belong to the art gallery or museum. The Air chair belongs in the everyday, public environment on a mass scale. Another member of the 'egosystem' to design for the mass market is Tom Dixon. An art-school drop out, he achieved celebrity status by his membership in a band and decorating environments with objects for the warehouse dance scene. He began by making furniture from found objects, and the 'cradle-to-cradle' or holistic approach of the sustainability design agenda has always informed his work. Conventionally, chair design – and any type of design – concentrates on the creation of something new without thought for the eventual destination of the object. With a new emphasis on sustainability, design now takes the beginning and end of production into account – integrating easy recycling and reuse, rather than destining the whole lot for the landfill site.

Tom Dixon's Kitchen chairs from 1987 consist of a welded, mild steel body augmented by real-life frying pans and soup ladles. He revels in welding and crafting objects from scratch. His 'S' chair, produced by the Italian firm Cappellini from 1987, is an elegant, sinuous form with a bent mild steel frame and covered in either woven cane, latex or rush. Dixon now works with Design Research Ltd and Artek, the Finnish modernist furniture company. Dixon did work for populist high street retailer Habitat in the 1990s into the 2000s – as Head of Design from 1998, then Creative Director from 2001 – and his popular touch has not diminished. At the 2006 London Design Fair he perpetrated the 'Chair Grab', when 500 polystyrene chairs were given away free to the general public. His interest in materials and sustainability was most prominent in the Fresh Fat project. Here, Dixon worked with plastic as a craft material, almost like clay, and moulded it into soft, translucent shapes.

Jasper Morrison, Air chair, 1999, providing seating at the café of Kingston University, London, where Morrison studied design.

Such an approach to the materiality of the craft of the chair and the sustainable agenda has informed the work of many chair designers since the early 1990s. Jakki Dehn's Niche armchair's exciting shape combines a traditional armchair on one side with an inglenook construction on the other. This means that there are a variety of sitting positions, with legs slung over the low arm, or curled up in a cosy ball in the niche. Importantly for the designer, the chair is covered in 100 per cent recycled polyester, sourced from Knoll in a Snowball print. The Picto office chair, made by the German furniture

Jakki Dehn, Niche armchair, upholstered in Knoll *Milkballs Wide Angle* from Studiotex, 100 per cent recycled polyester.

manufacturer Wilkhahn and designed by Produkt Entwicklung Roerick, is less innovative in terms of design form, but it is 90 per cent recyclable. The 'cradle-to-cradle' approach is exemplified in the Picto chair, which is designed clearly to distinguish the different materials used, from its aluminium frame to its polypropylene back and seat. The chair was also designed to be repaired easily, and has been in production since 1992.

An aesthetic of using obviously recycled materials in chair design also emerged in the 1990s. Jane Attfield, for example, created a simply shaped chair from processed chips derived from coloured plastic bottles. The RCP2 chair was manufactured by a UK-based company, Made of Waste, in 1994, using technology developed by an American company, Yemm & Hart in Missouri. The variety and blending of colours are the hallmarks of this chair, which is almost a manifesto in itself for using recycled plastics. A less unified effect is created by Bär & Knell's chair of 1990, made from abandoned plastic packaging which was draped over a frame, then melted to produce a *mélange* of distressed and distorted imagery to make a flowing surface, a molten mosaic of throw away plastic. A similarly fluid design is Marcel Wanders's Knotted chair of 1996. Ironically, the chair is made from neatly knotted rope which was then wound around carbon and then stiffened with epoxy resin. The chair grew out of the Dry Tech I project hosted by the Aviation and Space Lab at the Technical University at Delft in the Netherlands. It combined the rough and ready aesthetic of Droog Design with high-technology materials, and it is now on sale through Droog Design at an astonishing €1,970.

Droog Design was established in Amsterdam in 1993 and has introduced a more conceptual and political dimension to design. Founded by the art historian Renny Ramakers and the designer and teacher Gijs Bakker, it nurtured young designers to explore the limits of design, often using ironic twists. For example, Niels van Eijk created the Cow chair in 1997. This is literally made from one cowhide, which is soaked and then draped over a chair form and left to dry. The creative thinking of Droog Design can also present practical solutions. The delightful Highchair by Maartje Steenkamp of 2003 consists of a fairly conventional baby high chair in white beech. The ironic twist is that the chair can be altered to accommodate the growing child, with marks where the chair legs can be sawn off and the front restraint eventually removed to make a more child-friendly chair. A more literal use of recycled materials is the 1991 Rag chair by Tejo Remy. Some fifteen bags of discarded textiles are used in layers on a wooden frame, then bound by metal strips to create a seat full of memories and history. The owner also has the option of incorporating their own redundant materials into the chair, to make it an even more unique piece, now available through Droog Design at €3,200.

A mindfulness about materials has continued to inform the production and consumption of chairs into the twenty-first century. An air of comfort and understated luxury is evident in the hand-crafted Minx chair, designed in 2007 by Somerville Scott & Company. The American black walnut frame supports 100 per cent duck-feather cushions, covered in emerald-green mohair. Retailing at £3,400, this high-end chair is understated in its armchair profile. Less understated is Lee Broom's Neo Neon range. He picks out the familiar profile of traditional chair shapes with a strip of coloured neon light. The Electric Louis chair of 2007 consists of a Louis XIV chair shape, with a narrow, pink light profiling the back, arms and legs in pink neon, which reflects against the richly lacquered surfaces. The luxury goods design company and fashion house, English Eccentrics, also manipulate traditional chair forms and add their signature surface designs. Its recent Flocked chair of 2006 consists of a traditional, French shape which is then flocked – a process whereby hard surfaces are covered in a velvet-like surface. Different, vibrant colours are

available, including orange, electric blue and bright pink. The chair is then upholstered in silk in matching colourways. Another surprising juxtaposition of materials and form is achieved with a black patent leather beanbag offered for sale by the modernist furniture retailer Heal's. It is debatable whether the chair, more conventionally offered with a canvas covering, is 'A contemporary option for the home, perfect for jazzing up the living room or bedroom and for lounging on when watching the TV or chilling out.'[21] The chair is also available in gold leather.

Traditional French chair forms have also been reinvented for the burgeoning market of garden furniture. Dutch by Design was founded in 2003 by Venka de Rooij and exports fresh, new design from the Netherlands around the globe. In 2008 the firm marketed rubber-covered Baroque chairs in several colours for the garden. A more recent classic chair design, Arne Jacobsen's Egg chair, has been reissued as a garden chair with a range of different-coloured upholstery and a waterproof outer lining. Other cues from 1960s chair design have been used for garden furniture, including the Moon inflatable chair, which comes complete with its own pump. The Brazilian chair designers Fernando and Humberto Campana are directly inspired by materials and they recycled the usual plastic outdoor seating and combined it with a wicker outer frame. Scouring the streets and markets of São Paulo, they find and reuse discarded items to make surprising chairs – soft toys, rope and fabric strips, as in the case of the Sushi chair from 2003. It is manufactured by Edra, and the Campana brothers now also work with the Italian specialist design manufacturers Alessi. Entire chairs made from stuffed pandas or crocodiles have a great impact because of the materials employed. The makeshift, shanty towns of São Paulo, the *favelas*, were used as an inspiration for the title of a Campana brothers chair, constructed entirely from offcuts of wood in a haphazard manner. Priced now at $3,200 upwards, these chairs

Tejo Remy, Rag chair, 1991, for Droog Design.

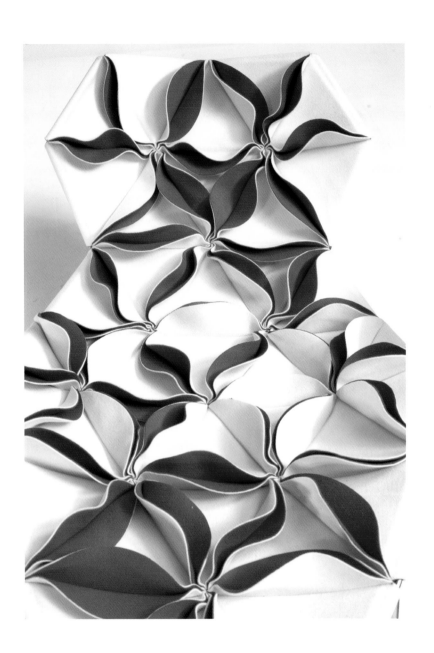

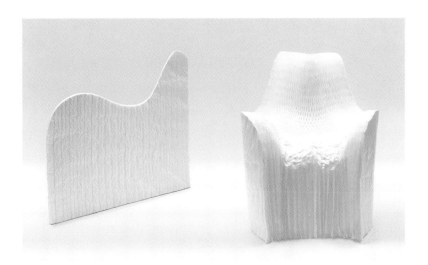

represent the irony of the artist's chair, reinvented from the deprived areas of Brazil and resold to the Western world's wealthy cognoscenti.

Chair designs such as these draw attention to the extreme poverty of most of the world's population and the stark contrast to the West's disproportionate ownership of resources but the issue of materials' scarcity and global warming affects everyone. After an explosion in outsourcing the production of furniture, most notably to China, Western furniture manufacturers are now seeking to produce their products nearer to home. This allows for greater quality control of the end product and a reduction in the carbon footprint. Conversely, bamboo has now entered the market as an ecologically friendly material: 'It's sustainable, versatile and attractive too – we're having a bamboo moment.'[22] Renewable and strong, most bamboo furniture is exported from Asia to the rest of the world. How issues of sustainability are factored into the extolled virtues of bamboo remains under debate, since our post 9/11 world faces economic downturn and increased scarcity of materials and energy.

Old materials, new chairs: Patricia Urquiola, Antibodi Chair, 2006, with felt and wool petals sewn into the leather seat. Tokujin Yoshioka Inc, Honey-pop Armchair, 2001. The honeycomb-paper construction opens concertina-like from a flat piece, taking its final form from the imprint of the sitter which creates the seat.

5 Fine Art Chairs

In a bizarre reversal of roles, designers have increasingly aspired to produce chairs that look like art, and fine artists have increasingly explored representations of the chair in their art. Artists have always used chairs to represent power and identity in painting and sculpture, especially in the genre of portraiture. This trend was later transposed into representing the human image in the new technology of photography. Artists' portraits of their own chairs have been used to represent their character and emotions – how they see themselves, represented through this most anthropomorphic of furniture pieces. And more recently, sculptors and installation artists have manipulated the form of the chair to create new meanings, exploiting the familiarity of this object in the gallery, museum space and beyond. Designers have celebrated the dissolution of barriers between art, design and craft by labelling their work 'Design Art' in exhibitions such as 'Telling Tales: Fantasy and Fear in Contemporary Design', held at the V&A Museum in 2009. High-profile artists, such as Damien Hirst, have designed their own version of the chair.

Traditionally, the painted portrait is the most usual site for the inclusion of a chair in fine art. There is an obviously functional reason why portraits represent individuals in a seated position, since the length of time taken to paint a portrait makes it more comfortable

Joseph Kosuth's *One and Three Chairs*, 1965. An artwork that includes the object, the words and the image.

for the subject, or quite literally, for the sitter, to sit. But, moreover, the cultural power and status represented by the chair also plays a significant part. As Joanna Woodall has argued:

> To take one example, the cleric was conventionally identifiable not only by his gorgeously rendered attire and ring of office but by the employment of a three-quarter-length, usually three-quarter view of the sitter enthroned in an upright, rectilinear chair. One might think, for example, of van Dyck's portrait of Cardinal Bentivoglio (1623) or Velazquez's image of Pope Leo X (1650).[1]

The seated portrait reinforced papal authority, displayed physically with the *Sedia Gestatoria*, a portable throne that was used to carry popes through the crowds on particularly important occasions, most notably a papal coronation. It is essentially a richly decorated, silk-covered armchair that is mounted on a platform with gilded rings on either side. Long poles are inserted through the rings, allowing twelve uniformed footmen to transport the pope on their shoulders. The whole effect is finished off by two large, white, ostrich-feather fans that frame the pope on either side of the chair. The *Sedia Gestatoria* allowed the crowds of faithful to view the pope from afar, and it is a tradition that lasted for a millennium until John Paul II refused to use it at his coronation in 1978 and instead adopted a less traditional, adapted motor car, or 'popemobile'.

The power behind the throne also informed the representation of the monarchy. Although the rulers did not use a specially adapted sedan chair, like the pope they were portrayed sitting in similarly, richly decorated, scarlet silk chairs to reinforce their divinely appointed authority. The portrait of Charles II (c. 1660–65) displays the king in his Garter robes, orb in hand, posing on a rectilinear scarlet and gold chair. This is the ruler of Great Britain at the time of the Restoration,

an imposing presence and all-powerful in a Protestant nation that had eschewed the authority of the Roman Catholic Church. Similarly, Chinese portraits of the Ming Dynasty (AD 1368–1644) represent the emperor seated, in luxurious robes with legs apart, almost straddling the empire. Such portraits were predominately of the male monarch, and portrayals of feminine subjects dealt with generalities, not individual identities. Most often shown as uniform, anonymous beauties, women rarely featured in individual portraits, revealing their status in society.

In terms of the exploitation of chairs in portraiture, by the eighteenth century, if women were depicted in a family portrait, they would be most often portrayed seated without the chair in view, concealed by voluminous skirts, or in mythical settings and poses whilst standing or reclining. For example, Jean Raoux's portrayal of *Ancient Virgins* (1727) depicts six Roman virgins clustered around the sacred

John Michael Wright or studio, *Charles II*, c. 1660–65.

flame, which they are destined to keep alight, in long flowing robes. None is shown seated, and their faces are indistinguishable from each other. Another example, George Romney's *Mr and Mrs William Lindow* (1772), depicts a wealthy couple made rich by the slave trade. He sits on a dark green upholstered chair; she stands by his side in a classical pose, the authority of the male reinforced by the presence of the chair. Similarly, Johan Zoffany's *David Garrick in 'The Farmer's Return'* (1762) depicts the actor sitting on an upright, high-backed, wooden chair, surrounded by two standing women and one boy.

This gender division continued into the nineteenth century; shifting patterns of power and hierarchy meant that portrait conventions used to depict heroes were adopted for the representation of leading political figures, professional thinkers and industrialists. All were shown in three-quarter or top-half only, seated in an authorita-

Jean Raoux, *Ancient Virgins*, 1727.

tive chair, perhaps surrounded by the trappings of their professional life. The portraits, usually in a limited palette of black, white and neutral shades, signified a subject worthy of respect and the influence invested in them by society. J. E. Millais's portrait of the great Victorian political thinker and writer Thomas Carlyle (1877) is a case in point. Depicted in black, greys and white, Carlyle is shown seated in a dining chair with arms. He rests his elbows there, his hands resting on a cane. He stares out at the viewer with a fixed gaze, confident in his intellectual ability and sense of individual worth and identity. By contrast, portraits of women predominately focused on the colourful and rich textiles of expansive skirts, details of decorative trimmings and hair arrangements, way beyond the conventions of contemporary fashion. Millais himself portrayed women floating in water with *Ophelia* (1851–2), kneeling in *Christ in the House of His Parents*

John Everett Millais, *Thomas Carlyle*, 1877.

(1849–50), standing and stretching in *Mariana* (1851) or tied naked to a tree in *Knight Errant* (1870). When Millais did paint women in a seated position, the chairs are barely visible beneath the frothy folds of the textiles, as in *Hearts Are Trumps* (1872).

Painted portraits were expensive and time-consuming to produce, and so only the social elite was immortalized in paint before the mid-nineteenth century, to be viewed by an equally select audience. This changed with the opening of public galleries – for example, the National Portrait Gallery in London in 1856 – bringing portraits to the masses. Mass-circulation illustrated magazines, such as the *Illustrated London News* (launched in 1842), also featured portraits. These were in the form of engravings, usually taken from paintings or early photographs, of the great and the good. These worthies were usually pictured in the conventional three-quarter-length pose, seated

John Everett Millais, *Hearts Are Trumps,* 1872.

in an authoritative chair, and they were usually male. The advent of photography revolutionized the social spread of who could appear in a portrait, the mechanization of image-making resulting in a much cheapter process. Portrait studios proliferated and often used a chair as a prop, particularly since the exposure time could be lengthy so the sitter needed to keep completely still. My paternal grandmother was photographed in a studio in 1916 at the age of three, actually standing on such a chair – a reproduction of a Jacobean oak original. As the daughter of a Durham coal miner, she is portrayed in her Sunday best, enjoying the novel experience of having her photograph taken, just like millions of others like her.

With the increased availability of the camera and the mass development of the family photograph, the construction of the portrait became far more informal. Chairs appeared in family photographs as

A toddler posed on a reproduction 17th-century chair in an early 20th-century studio portrait: Violet Green, the author's paternal grandmother, England, 1916.
The chair as a prop in another early 20th-century studio portrait.

part of the general domestic ensemble. The chair no longer denoted prestige or status, only domestic comfort. In one photograph my late husband sits in his home in the late 1970s, complete with Draylon-covered armchair, mantelpiece ornaments and family dog. A fleeting moment fixed indefinitely; an image of domesticity and belonging, a self-portrait, taken by an amateur photographer, taken by himself.

The recognition of photography as an art form was slow to emerge, since within the traditional hierarchy of culture it occupied a lower position than that of painting. However, from the 1920s onwards the

Edouard Manet, *Emile Zola*, 1868.

medium became accepted, at least in avant-garde circles, as equal to that of painting. Despite this democratization of portraiture through technology in the West, the painted portrait retained its cachet as a method of presenting a higher-status image of the self. The convention of showing the sitter posed in a chair remained the norm. In avant-garde art, painters used the chair to explore form and meaning of the two-dimensional picture surface, using mundane and everyday subject matter. The portrait becomes less a representation of a type – be it cleric or autocrat – and more particularized as a distinct individual. This is reflected in the chairs depicted by painters, for example *Emile Zola* (1868) by the French realist Edouard Manet, which shows the writer amidst the fashionable Japanese trappings of the painter's studio. Therefore, he sits on a particular chair, the upholstery represented by orange and black swirling brushstrokes and the upholstery nails picked out in gold against black. The Impressionists were more likely to paint the outdoors, with picnickers or Sunday strollers sitting on the grass, than interior scenes or conventional portraits. One exception to this were the Nabis, a group of Parisian artists who delighted in painting interior scenes, usually of their own domestic spaces. Pierre Bonnard, for example, painted sun-bathed, golden interiors featuring his wife and children and modest furniture, including the kitchen table and the tin bath. It was Vincent van Gogh who took painting the personal in the form of the humble domestic chair to new levels, with *Van Gogh's Chair* (c. 1888).

Van Gogh painted the chair at Arles in the south of France during the time of the turbulent visit by a fellow artist, Paul Gauguin. A simple peasant's chair in roughly hewn wood with rush seating sits on the uneven, terracotta tiled floor. Placed on the seat is the artist's pipe and crumpled paper, as if he has just stood up and placed these objects on the seat. The canvas depicts only the chair, apparently boxed in by the encroaching walls, and testifies to Van Gogh's increasing

alienation from the world and from other people, even from his close collaborator, Gauguin. He wrote to his brother Theo:

> I am often terribly melancholy, irritable, hungering and thirsting, as it were, for sympathy; and when I do not get it, I try to act indifferently, speak sharply, and often even pour oil on fire. I do not like to be in company, and often find it painful and difficult to mingle with people, to speak with them . . . [2]

Van Gogh painted *Gauguin's Chair* at the same time, which is in stark contrast to his own. It was painted at night, as opposed to the bright sunlight of his own chair, shown by the lit candle on the seat of the chair and the gaslight on the wall. Gauguin's chair lacks the rustic primitivism of rush and pale wood, but is a far more ornate dark wood. It is shown resting on a patterned carpet, as opposed to tiling. Both chairs feature objects on their seats, Van Gogh's a pipe and paper, Gauguin's a candle and modern novels, perhaps symbolizing the discomfort of both men in Arles at that time – neither able to settle and work harmoniously individually or with one another. These two paintings summarize the lasting quality of the chair to symbolize and almost immortalize its owner, to represent and characterize the distinct qualities of the individual in ways that other pieces of furniture or objects cannot. Perhaps it is the anthropomorphic form of the chair, or its intimacy to the sitter's body, that creates this effect, added to the long-standing cultural importance of the chair as a powerful object.

The chair has been used in a similar way in film and on television to represent an individual character – Pip dances with a chair and imagines it is Estella in David Lean's 1946 adaptation of Charles Dickens's *Great Expectations*, and the Duplass brothers' comedy, *The Puffy Chair* (2005), follows the road trip of two brothers as they

Vincent van Gogh, *Van Gogh's Chair*, 1888. The chair as the artist.

attempt to deliver an old recliner chair, purchased from eBay, to their father in Atlanta. The chair is a replica of a La-Z-Boy once owned by their father, and represents the paternal figure throughout the film. Similarly, in the US TV series *Sex and the City*, Carrie Bradshaw's ex and furniture designer, Aiden Shaw, is represented by a chair he made himself that stands, unoccupied, in her flat, a reminder of the emptiness of their relationship.

The empty chair was again powerfully represented by the British artist Louise Pickard in *The Green Balcony*. The little wicker chair stands alone in the liminal space between house and garden; an absent presence is mournfully presented. Gwen John's soulful work, *A Corner of the Artist's Room in Paris (With Open Window),* shows

Louise Pickard, *The Green Balcony*, c. 1927.

her attic room at 87 Rue du Cherche-Midi. At the time, she was supporting herself by working as an artist's model and was in the throes of
an intense relationship with the sculptor Rodin. The chair is distinctly
the artist's own, with its dainty, pale wicker framework and abandoned
clothing. The vibrant blue dress represents the painter's vulnerability,
as she sat in her room, awaiting the arrival of her lover. Although
Rodin paid for her accommodation, his visits to the painter's room

Gwen John, *A Corner of the Artist's Room in Paris (With Open Window)*, 1907–9.

became less and less frequent, so she sat pining, and waiting for his infrequent calls, painting her domestic surroundings to vent her emotions. The open book beneath the open window, revealing the clear blue sky beyond, perhaps hints at her longing for escape and foretells her eventual interest in Catholicism.

This deeply personal image is in direct contrast to a conventional portrait by her more celebrated brother, Augustus John. *Madame Suggia* (1920–23) is a large (1.87 × 1.65 m / 6.14 × 5.40 ft) and flamboyant portrait of the celebrity solo cellist. She sits on an ornate Louis XVI-style gold and blue chair, mainly obscured by yards of her deep crimson dress. She holds the cello between her knees, but this pose is again hidden by the volume of textiles. This is a conventional pose, using the chair very much within the conventions of portraiture. A far more relaxed and provocative exploitation of the chair is used in the renowned photograph of Christine Keeler by Lewis Morley

Augustus John, *Madame Suggia*, 1920–23.

Christine Keeler, photograph by Lewis Morley, 1963.

(1963). The famous image was captured in the Soho studio of Morley, situated above the anti-establishment revue club *The Establishment*. The photographer was commissioned to provide images of Keeler for a forthcoming film. The film was never released and the titillating image was stolen and appeared in the *Sunday Mirror* without the photographer's consent. Keeler was reluctant to be photographed nude, but the film producers who were at the photo session insisted. Morley placed her in a pose he had used himself during the previous year. The pose, sitting astride a chair, maintained Keeler's modesty, but hinted at her nudity.

The chair as a framing device for the portrait is striking because of the contrast between the hard plywood and the soft, female flesh. It is a design based on a modernist icon, Arne Jacobsen's Model 3107 chair of 1955. However, it is more crude in shape, with a much narrower 'waist' and has an additional cut-out in its back for a handle. The photographer bought a set of six of the chairs from Heal's furniture shop in London in 1962, and the iconic status of the object has recently been confirmed with its acquisition by the V&A. The original designer of this chair has not been identified, and the V&A, where the chair is now kept, describes it as a 'knock off'.[3] It is signed on the base by the photographer, who has also confirmed that it was used to shoot photographs of Keeler, David Frost, Joe Orton and, more recently, Dame Edna Everage (Barry Humphries). And the pose has been used again and again, most recently by Homer in *The Simpsons*.

Another representation of 'Swinging London' that incorporates a modernist design icon is David Hockney's *Mr and Mrs Clark and Percy* (1970–71). This is a dual portrait of the fashion designer Ossie Clark and his partner, textile designer and long-term muse of Hockney, Celia Birtwell. She is pregnant and stands with lilies to her right, a symbol of pregnancy and the Annunciation. Ossie sits dishevelled and barefoot on a Breuer's Cesca cantilever chair. The flowing lines

of the chair in black and chrome are echoed by the languid limbs of Ossie, who holds a cigarette in one hand and a cat on one thigh. Although the couple had recently married, and Hockney was the best man, they appear glum and reserved, perhaps foreshadowing the breakdown of their relationship four years later. Other modernist, iconic chairs to appear in British artists' work at this time include Richard Hamilton's *Interior II* of 1964, which was part of a whole series of collaged images exploring the interior, produced in the mid-1960s. In *Interior II*, the Eameses' La Fonda chair is seen from behind; using thin aluminium Hamilton represents the back of the chair. Shaped balsa wood that was flocked in bright red was used to repre-

Richard Hamilton, *Interior II*, 1964.

sent the seat. The fabricated image protrudes from the surface of the picture plane. This immediately makes the iconic chair the focal point of the painting, since it interrupts the spectator's space. The black legs of the chair were a direct appropriation of the original image, and drips of paint run down the side of the chair. The photograph was taken from the Hille catalogue for the Herman Miller collection, demonstrating Hamilton's continued interest in modern design. He was working with the image of the interior, as he realized: 'I was very conscious of the fact that any interior is a set of anachronisms, a museum. The more "modern" treatment of *Interior II* tries to press home this point'.[4] Hamilton used the quintessential image of the modern chair to represent contemporary design, in contrast to the 1940s New Look outfit worn by Patricia Knight in a publicity still for the 1949 film *Shockproof*. The rapid changes in design styles and fashionability fascinated Hamilton at the time, and permeated his artwork of the 1960s.

Other Western artists have explored their signature themes, and incorporated chairs into their work. The sculptor Christo produced a *Wrapped Chair* in 1961 that consisted of a standard wooden chair partially covered in a dirty sheet and tied with rope. Robert Rauschen-berg's *Pilgrim* (1960) consists of a multi-coloured, abstract canvas with a painted wooden chair in the foreground. Claes Oldenburg's *Shirt With Objects on a Chair* (1962) again used a standard wooden chair with a plastered shirt hanging on the back, with a tie under-neath and an open wallet and small objects on the seat. So the mundane object of the chair has been taken, appropriated by the sculptor, to create an artwork with the addition of other materials. This unex-pected juxtaposition of the everyday and fine art jolts the viewer's perceptions. *Fat Chair* (1964) by the German artist Joseph Beuys uses a mundane, wooden chair that has a piece of fat in a wedge shape on the seat. Beuys became fascinated with the materials of fat and felt in the early 1960s, and used them to represent the spiritual and the chaos of the everyday. Here, fat symbolizes the materiality of the body with all the other substances removed. The use of such a volatile material also challenges our preconceptions about the permanence of the artwork, fat being solid at one temperature and liquid at another.

Joseph Kosuth's *One and Three Chairs* (1965) consists of a real chair, a photograph of a chair and a dictionary definition of the word chair. An example of conceptual art, the piece consisted of a set of instructions for the installer, which was to source a chair, take a photo of it, blow it up to the same size as the chair, and display the enlarged dictionary definition of the word 'chair' beside it. As the artist explained:

> I used common, functional objects – such as a chair – and to the left of the object would be a full-scale photograph of it and to the right of the object would be a photostat of a definition of the object from the dictionary. Everything you saw when you looked at the object had to be the same that you saw in the photograph, so each time the work was exhibited the new installation necessitated a new photograph. I liked that the work itself was something other than simply what you saw. By changing the location, the object, the photograph and still having it remain the same work was *very* interesting. It meant you could have an art work which was that *idea* of an art work, and its formal components weren't important.[5]

In all these cases, the ordinary chair – the more mundane the better – has been used to explore the boundaries of what fine art practice is. The chair is an ideal object for this purpose, the most easily identifiable of household objects with which we, in the West, have an intimate relationship. Possibly one of the most controversial uses of a chair in modern Western art has been Edwin and Nancy Reddin Kienholz's *Bear Chair* (1991). A model of a semi-naked girl is tied beneath the chair, with her head resting on the back of the seat. A model bear with an erect penis stands on the chair, looking in a dressing-table mirror with the words '*IF YOU EVER TELL I'LL HURT YOUR MAMA REAL REAL BAD*' inscribed on the top of the dressing table. A hard-hitting exposé of child abuse and hypocrisy, the installation aims and succeeds in shocking the spectator, the normality of the chair and the fairy-tale connotations of the bear adding to the horror of the artwork. So the title of the piece, and the shock of seeing a familiar, household piece of furniture implicated in a horrific act, problematizes our accepted ideas of the mundane chair.

Whilst these artists appropriated existing chairs as a crucial part of their artwork, the British pop artist Allen Jones created a three-dimensional sculpture based on a chair but in human form, with the body of a woman transfigured into the form of a chair. Slightly larger than life, the sculpture was produced in an edition of six by Gems Wax Models to the specifications of the artist. *Chair* was part of a 1969 series that also included *Hatstand* and *Table.* The highly sexualized pose of *Chair*, with the model lying on her back and bent double, with her legs pressing against her breasts, is further reinforced by her black, knee-length stiletto boots laced up at the back, elbow-length black gloves and black knickers, which define her buttocks. The fibreglass body has a seat strapped to it, formed from perspex with a stuffed, black leather cushion resting on it. The erotic S&M overtones are further enhanced by the highly made-up face of the model, with half-closed eyes and obvious wig. Intimacy and eroticism are signalled by placing the piece on a tactile sheepskin rug. The sexual fetish of objectifying women to perform as furniture is known as Forniphilia.

For Allen Jones, the sculpture was erotic and aimed to reach out to everyone, whether a modern art expert or not. Artfully naive, Jones ignores feminist objections to the erotic objectification of women, and argues: 'The erotic impulse transcends cerebral barriers and demands a direct emotional response . . . It seems to me a democratic idea that art should be accessible to everyone on some level, and eroticism in one such level.'[6]

However, feminist scholars at the time found the piece degrading to women in its overt objectification. In 1973 Laura Mulvey applied a Freudian reading to Jones's work in the women's liberation magazine *Spare Rib* and described the discomfort of fetish clothing: 'The most effective fetish both constricts, and up-lifts, binds and raises, particularly high-heeled shoes, corsets and bras.'[7] Lisa Tickner contributed a piece on Allen Jones to the first issue of the critical theory journal *Block* in 1979. Tickner put forward a more subtle argument, claiming that Jones was exploring existing popular representations of women, but she did not perceive this as politically neutral, as the artist did: 'the exploitation of already exploitative material cannot be seen as politically neutral, whatever the artist's intentions and the use of a particular kind of sexual imagery contributes to the . . . degradation of women'.[8]

This feminist perspective acted as an important critique of stereotypical views of women as sex objects. However, in the more complex and changed landscape of the twenty-first century, sado-masochist sex practices have been re-examined critically, and there is a broader acceptance of different sexual proclivities in society in general. In a recent analysis of pornography and art, Kelly Dennis calls for a multitude of non-judgemental approaches: 'Rather than establish a singular teleology for pornography, I draw on a "constellation" of methods to approach the seemingly disparate discourses of art and porn.'[9] The growing acceptability of pornography by the mainstream is evidenced in bondage clothing, which inspired Punk clothing, boned corsets now worn as outerwear by top celebrities such as Cheryl Cole, Lady Gaga and Katy Perry. Rubber clothing is losing its *outré* appeal, and is worn to go clubbing. The sales of corsets have almost doubled in the past year, with the mainstream British department store Selfridges reporting a 70 per cent increase in sales.[10] A recent issue of *Wallpaper** magazine, for example, was devoted to sex and featured the apartment where the graphic designer Peter Saville lived throughout the late 1990s.[11] The 1970s-style apartment is billed as 'the perfect set for a very modern playboy'.[12] Saville collaborated with the fashion photographer Nick Knight to create a series of room settings entitled 'in every dream home'.[13] In the feature we see female models arranged in various erotic poses and wearing rubber and leather, including an Allen Jones-inspired pair of legs in extraordinarily high shoes. There is also a bondage table, a fetishistic revolving wheel and a stretching rack on the top of a confinement cage. It all seems strangely acceptable now. But the acceptability rests on an ambiguity: the women are not secured by the bondage devices; they stand near them. Perhaps the intention is that the spectator or photographer is destined to be restrained by the dominant women. The striking sets are sprinkled with modernist chairs, for example, Gaetano Pesce's Up 5 and Up 6 armchair and ottoman, now marketed by B&B Italia. This alludes to the slightly edgy, fetishistic underlying theme that has always existed in modernist chair design – cruelly contorting the body into unnatural poses to please the modern designer.

Artists have pushed back the boundaries of acceptability not only in terms of sex and sexuality in relation to the chair, but also in relation to death. As I have found myself, death is the last taboo in Western society. Nobody wants to talk about it. I have stopped dinner party conversations in their tracks by mentioning I am a widow. No one knows what to say, or how to respond. We have lost the certainty of religion and the strict moral codes of the Victorian era. Andy Warhol flatly represented death in his reworked images of the car crash and the electric chair. The chair, starkly standing in isolation, in rough black and white or coloured form, the ultimate symbol of premeditated, deliberate killing and execution on behalf of society. Warhol began using the image of the electric chair in his work from 1963 onwards, the year in which the last two executions by this method took place in New York State. He continued to explore this theme over the next ten years in his paintings and prints.

Whilst feminists critiqued the work of artists like Allen Jones, women artists have worked with the form of the chair to represent the familiar, or the over-familiar. The British bad-girl artist Tracey Emin has taken familiar objects, most infamously a tent, and reworked them to express her life history. In *There's a Lot of Money in Chairs* (1994) she took a chair originally owned by her grandmother and embroidered it while she journeyed between San Francisco and New York in 1994. During the road trip she sat in the chair and read excerpts from her autobiography, *Exploration of the Soul* (1994). The tiny, bucket chair was decorated with 'OK PUDDIN, THANKS PLUM', appliquéd across the front of the seat, referring to nicknames between the two, with their two dates of birth together with that of Emin's twin brother. She embroidered the chair with the stopping places during the journey, including San Diego, Death Valley and Detroit. So the chair began as a performance prop, underwent the process of craft-working by the artist, to end up displayed in a glass case in galleries, first at the White Cube, London, and then at her retrospective at the Scottish National Gallery of Modern Art in 2008. Another British installation artist, Sally Spinks, has taken a chair to act as a potent symbol of memory and family. *Home Sick Home 2* (2008) takes an abandoned chair, with ripped upholstery and arms, without a cushion. She then created three pieces of machine-knitted patches in the form of traditional tattoos – the bluebird, skull and crossbones, and the heart – and sewed them over the rips. Spinks states:

> I was working with tattoo imagery that I believe has a connection to comfort in a chaotic post-modern world rather than the old class rooted

associations of tattoos in the past (in UK culture) and I used a number of home 'comfort' items to work with such as the chair and carpets. The chair itself is old, the cushion missing and the material ripped so I produced machine knitted tattoo emblems which are stitched over the rips as if to repair the chair and restore its comfort much as a person perhaps does in getting their body tattooed.[14]

So, if comfort is the theme of *Home Sick Home 2*, then the delineation of public space into private space is the theme of Cat Bagg's piece *This Land is my Land* (2009). Situated beneath a section of Black-friars Bridge on the north bank of the Thames, the illuminated chair

Sally Spinks, *Home Sick Home 2*, 2008.

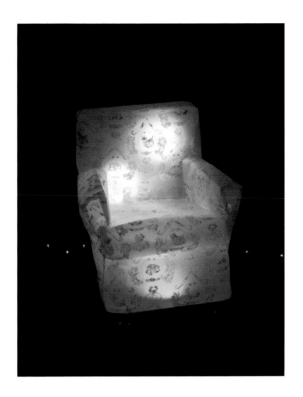

is surrounded by a ring of earth and white fairy lights. This temporary piece of public art makes a statement about the chair's ability to
create barriers, whereas the work of the Austrian artist Hans Schabus
explores the ordering power of the chair.

Schabus created an installation at the Barbican Art Gallery, London,
in 2008 on the theme of the chair. Entitled *Next Time I'm Here, I'll Be
There*, he imitated the layout of a large commercial aeroplane on the
gallery's 80 m (262 ft) wall, known as The Curve. The artist secured
a total of 461 chairs at a 90-degree angle on the wall, arranged
according to the layout of seats on an aircraft. The chairs were all
sourced from chairs owned by the Barbican Centre, and so consist-

Cat Bagg, *This Land is my Land*, part of the Hive T1 + 2 Gallery urban intervention series
'999 – Requiem to a Bridge', London, 2009.

ed of standard, upholstered conference and computer chairs as well as the Arne Jacobsen 3107 model. Schabus produced the piece to reflect the orderliness and controlled nature of modern life, as represented by the chair. As explained in the accompanying catalogue, *Take A Seat*:

> Chairs play a crucial role in our civilization. The sitting position is so closely connected to our everyday lives that we are confronted with seating in every situation we encounter. We connect both physically and psychologically with the chairs we choose, and not only do they provide us with comfort, and help us to cope with our daily routine, but they place us within the disciplined hierarchy of human life. Chairs position us in a fixed frame, circumscribe distances and generate patterns of encounter, bringing people together, creating intimacy within groups, and influencing our actions, sensations and behaviour.[15]

Other artists to use the everyday chair to critique society include the Colombian installation artist Doris Salcedo. During 2002 she spent two days lowering 280 chairs in front of the Palace of Justice in Bogotá, blurring the boundaries between installation and performance art. The number of chairs represented the number of people killed in the guerilla coup of 1985. In 2003, at the 8th Istanbul Biennial, Salcedo used ordinary chairs again, and completely filled in a derelict building plot with 1,550 of them. This time the wooden chairs represented the plight of anonymous migrants, who sustain the globalized economy. The chairs are heaped randomly, one on top of the other, and reach the tops of the buildings on either side. They are also level with the facades and punctuate the urban space in a surprising and unexpected way.

If contemporary artists have excelled in critiquing society through the device of the chair, they have also been involved in redesigning it. The British artist Damien Hirst designed a butterfly-print deckchair in 2008. Based on the butterfly image of his *All You Need Is Love, Love, Love* limited-edition screen print of the same year, the deckchair comes in six colourways with a timber frame. The price tag of £300 or £500 for two is justified by the addition of a stainless-steel plaque, bearing the artist's signature on the deckchair frame. And it is an unlimited edition.

The blurring of boundaries between art and design, the artist and designer, is reflected in the exhibition of the chair in museums and galleries. The V&A, previously a bastion of traditional values where contemporary design would never have been encountered amongst the precious ecclesiastical silver, hosted 'Telling Tales: Fantasy and Fear in Contemporary Design' (2009). Curated by Gareth Williams, the show consisted of different environments grouped around the themes of 'The Forest Glade', 'The Enchanted Castle' and 'Heaven and Hell'. The show deliberately set out to challenge expectations of what could be seen at the V&A by featuring 'Design Art, a catch-all term for objects that are somewhere between art, craft and design'.[16] It featured the work of mainly young Dutch artists such as Tord Boontje, who showed the Princess chair, a white antique chair dressed with a white bride's veil, a train of light pink flowers and white ruffs masking the chair legs. This Cinderella object is contrasted with Boontje's Witch, a curved chair covered in black leather scales with a bright red lining beneath the seat of the chair. This contrast between absolute evil and naive goodness lies at the heart of many traditional fairy-tales, and the show itself. Concentrating on the theme of the narrative and the myth was a neat device to exhibit chairs that told stories, rather than being objects designed to sit on. Fairy-tales frequently feature chairs as part of the narrative, including 'The Three Bears' and 'Little Red Riding Hood'. Nestled in the dark setting of a fairy-tale wood, 'The Forest Glade' with its rustling trees and dim lighting evoked the world of childhood fantasies and scary stories. The most literal manifestation of Design

Art could be glimpsed in 'The Enchanted Castle' section with the *Venus and Mars* piece of 2006. The Russian-born designer Constantin Boym worked with his partner, Laurene Leon Boym, and used a cheap reproduction of the Veronese masterpiece, slicing two thirds of the image to cover a simple chair, and leaving the remaining third on a mirror behind. The Boyms are designers who bite back, who challenge the recent trend for artists to design chairs; they are designers who work with art. As Constantin Boym professed:

> When design becomes art, there is a possibility of re-imagining the object in a very different and radical way. Like in painting, cinema or literature, life itself becomes the theme of the designer's work. The chair could be about love, or war, or death, or disaster – and not necessarily about the comfort of sitting. The subject of design expands to such a degree that we can only imagine the possibilities that lie ahead.[17]

The tables have been turned at the Serpentine Gallery, London, with its first exhibition of contemporary design. Whilst the V&A gravitated towards designers who produced one-off art, the Serpentine in its 2009–10 'Design Real' show invited the product designer Konstantin Grcic to curate an exhibition devoted to functional, mass-produced design. The 43 objects on display in the gallery are simple, functional and ordinary. The category of 'Office Chair' is represented by Herman Miller's Aeron and 'Chair' by Jasper Morrison's Air chair. The ambition to celebrate affordable design is to be applauded, but surely design deserves better analysis and research than a cut-and-paste from commercial websites and Wikipedia on the exhibition website, www.design-real.com. There is no hint of the psychological appeal of design, the emotional or the narrative that the V&A explored so well.

A chair that realizes the potential power of the chair form is the Throne of Weapons made in 2001 by a Mozambique-based artist,

Doris Salcedo, *Untitled*, 2003, installation in Karakoy, Istanbul, for the 8th International Istanbul Biennial.

Kester. The piece was created as part of a Christian Aid project called TAE – Transformaçaõ de Armas em Enxadas (Transforming Arms into Tools) – which funded the exchange of weapons previously used by soldiers on both sides of the Mozambique civil war. Weapons were swapped for tools and the Throne was made from these unwanted weapons, including a Russian AK47 rifle. The piece is now owned by the British Museum, which had bought it from a Christian Aid exhibition entitled 'Swords into Ploughshares: Transforming Arms into Art' in 2002. It carries an important pacifist and environmentally friendly message about the creative possibilities of recycling. A chair with a message.

So the chair as an object in society and in culture has permeated every nuance of its structuring. Chairs still represent authority, whether the authority of the sitter or the authority of the person controlling the sitter. The form of the chair is so intrinsic to Western culture that every discipline of visual and material culture – design, craft, decorating and fine art – as well as the consumer has contact with it. The structure of the book has mirrored these different disciplines. However, just as I write the closing words, I realize that, of course, barriers between disciplines are being eroded, being questioned, being transgressed. But this was a start. The book reveals and illuminates the meaning of the chair as it has weathered the storms of history and remains with us today. But with the convergence of technologies and the blurring of boundaries, who knows what may happen next? Or we may welcome the allure of the comfy chair, to escape the demands of the world out there. And I bet you are reading this book while sitting on one.

References

Introduction

1 See Galen Cranz, *The Chair: Rethinking Culture, Body, and Design* (London, 1998).
2 Leora Auslander, *Taste and Power: Furnishing Modern France* (London, 1996), pp. 18–19.
3 Stua advertisement as featured in *Wallpaper* magazine (December 2009), p. 108.

1 Seats of Power

1 *Chambers Dictionary of Etymology* (Edinburgh, 1988), p. 157.
2 Ian McEwan, *On Chesil Beach* (London, 2008), p. 5.
3 Amin Jaffer, 'Indian Princes and the West', in A. Jackson and A. Jaffer, eds, *Maharaja: The Splendour of India's Royal Courts* (London, 2009), p. 196.
4 Sigfried Giedion, *Mechanization Takes Command: A Contribution to Anonymous History* (London, 1969), pp. 269–70.
5 As quoted in Florence de Dampierre, *Chairs: A History* (New York, 2006), pp. 154–5.
6 Markman Ellis, *The Coffee House: A Cultural History* (London, 2004), p. 59.
7 Thomas Chippendale, *The Gentleman and Cabinetmaker's Directory* (London, 1754), p. 8.
8 George Hepplewhite, *The Cabinet-Maker and Upholsterer's Guide*, 3rd edn (London 1897), unpaginated.
9 Doris Elizabeth King, 'The First-Class Hotel and the Age of the Common Man', *Journal of Southern History*, XXIII/2 (May 1957), p. 177.
10 Charles Maurice de Talleyrand-Périgord, as quoted in Dampierre, *Chairs*, p. 271.
11 See Jan Marsh, 'Votes for Women and Chastity for Men: Gender, Health, Medicine and Sexuality', in John M. MacKenzie, ed., *The Victorian Vision: Inventing New Britain* (London, 2001), p. 99.
12 Charles L. Eastlake, *Hints on Household Taste*, reprint of 1878 4th revd edn (New York, 1986), p. vi.

13 Ibid., pp. 162–3.

14 Juliet Kinchin, 'Interiors: Nineteenth-century Essays on the "Masculine" and the "Feminine" Room', in Pat Kirkham, *The Gendered Object* (Manchester, 1996), p. 12.

15 Walter Benjamin, *The Arcades Project*, trans. H. Eiland and L. McLaughlin (London, 1999), pp. 8–9.

16 The painting is in the National Galleries of Scotland, and can be viewed online.

17 Jean Baudrillard, 'Structures of Interior Design' (1968), reprinted in Ben Highmore, ed., *The Everyday Life Reader* (London, 2002), p. 309.

18 Friedrich Engels, *Die Lage der arbeitenden Klasse in England*, 2nd edn (Leipzig, 1848), pp. 36–7, as quoted in Walter Benjamin, *The Arcades Project*, pp. 427–8.

19 See Adrian Forty, *Objects of Desire: Design and Society, 1750–1980* (London, 1986), pp. 67–72.

20 Ibid., pp. 129–30.

21 Fiona Fisher, 'Privacy and Supervision in the Modernised Public House, 1872–1902', in *Designing the Modern Interior*, ed. P. Sparke, A. Massey and B. Martin (London, 2009), pp. 41–52.

22 Christoph Grafe and Franziska Bollerey, eds, *Cafes and Bars: The Architecture of Public Display* (London, 2008), p. 12.

23 Annette Kuhn, *Cinema Culture in 1930s Britain: End of Award Report* (unpublished, 1997).

24 Blake Morrison, *And When Did You Last See Your Father?* (Manchester, 1993), p. 19.

25 R. Roberts, *The Classic Slum* (Manchester, 1971), p. 75.

26 Harold Pinter, excerpts from *The Homecoming* (London, 1991), reprinted in D. Neale, ed., *A Creative Writing Handbook* (London, 2009), p. 329.

27 Jonathan Franzen, *The Corrections* (London, 2001), pp. 8–9.

28 Leora Auslander, *Taste and Power: Furnishing Modern France* (London, 1996), p. 19.

2 The Designer's Presence

1 Peter York, 'Talking Chairs', *Design*, October 1988, p. 56.

2 Editorial, *Design* magazine (February 1970), p. 48.

3 Rosalind E. Krauss, 'The Originality of the Avant-Garde', in *The Originality of the Avant-Garde and Other Modernist Myths* (London, 1985), pp. 151–94. See also Nancy Troy, *Couture Culture: A Study in Modern Art and Fashion* (London, 2003), and Walter Benjamin, 'The Work of Art in the Age of Mechanical Reproduction', in *Illuminations*, trans. Harry Zohn (London, 1977), pp. 217–51.

4 See www.barcelonachair.com/knoll (accessed 28 November 2008).

5 Paul Overy, 'Carpentering the Classic: A Very Peculiar Practice. The Furniture of Gerrit Rietveld', *Journal of Design History*, IV/3 (1991), p. 139.

6 Peter Smithson, *The Cantilever Chair* [1986], as quoted in *The Modern Chair* (London, 1988), p. 4.

7 Mies van der Rohe, *Time* magazine (18 February 1957), as quoted on www.architecture.about.com.
8 As quoted in Christopher Wilk, *Marcel Breuer: Furniture and Interiors* (New York, 1981), p. 38.
9 Ibid., p. 70.
10 Le Corbusier, *Towards a New Architecture*, trans. Frederick Etchells, reprinted and enlarged from the 1931 edition (London, 1987), p. 227.
11 Gay McDonald, 'Selling the American Dream: Mo MA, Industrial Design and Postwar France', *Journal of Design History*, XVII/4 (2004), pp. 397–412. See also Mary Anne Staniszewski, *The Power of Display: A History of Exhibition Installations at the Museum of Modern Art* (Cambridge, 1998).
12 See Pat Kirkham, *Charles and Ray Eames: Designers of the Twentieth Century* (Cambridge, MA, and London, 1995), p. 210.
13 Ibid., p. 231.
14 KnollStudio, *Eero Saarinen Collection* brochure (2009), p. 2.
15 Ibid.
16 Gordon Russell, as quoted in 'Utility', *Design* magazine (September 1974), p. 64.
17 See 'Utility', *Design* magazine (September 1974), p. 66.
18 See Judy Attfield, *Utility Reassessed: The Role of Ethics in the Practice of Design* (Manchester, 2002); Anne Massey and Paul Micklethwaite, 'Unsustainability: Towards a New Design History', *Journal of Design Philosophy*, forthcoming.
19 Gordon Russell, 'On Buying Furniture', in *Daily Mail Year Book, 1953–4* (London,1953), p. 61.
20 David Nicholls, 'Hatching the Egg: Arne Jacobsen's Egg Chair Turned 50 this Year, Yet its Witty, Appealing Design Has Never Been More Popular', *Telegraph Magazine* (17 May 2008), p. 87.
21 Alison and Peter Smithson, 'Eames' Dreams', *Changing the Art of Inhabitation* (London, 1994), pp. 73–4; as quoted in Victoria Walsh, *Nigel Henderson: Parallel of Life and Art* (London, 2001), p. 116.
22 Reyner Banham, 'The Chair as Art', *New Society* (20 April 1967), p. 22.
23 Ibid., p. 20.
24 Clement Meadmore, *The Modern Chair: Classics in Production* (London, 1974), p. 9.
25 *Sit!*, exh. cat., RIBA, London (1982), p. 1.
26 Ibid., p. 9.
27 Kajuiter, 'The story of vitra. about the Eames Lounge Chair': http://www.desig naddict.com/design_addict/forums/index.cfm/fuseaction/thread_show_one/ thread_id/5649 (accessed 27 November 2009).

3 Luxury and Comfort

1 See John E. Crowley, *The Invention of Comfort: Sensibilities and Design in Early Modern Britain and Early America* (Baltimore and London, 2001).

2 Ibid., p. 146.

3 Thomas Pumphrey, *Gleanings of the Pumphrey Family, 1835–1908* (1907–8), Tyne and Wear Archives Service (1141/8). On display at the Geffrey Museum exhibition *Choosing the Chintz* (London, 2008–9).

4 *The American Heritage Dictionary of the English Language*, 4th edn (Boston, MA, 2008).

5 John Gloag, 'Smoker out of Windsor', *Connoisseur*, 190 (1979), p. 169.

6 Elizabeth Kendall, *House into Home* (London, 1962), p. 7.

7 Ibid., p. 53.

8 Sigfried Giedion, *Mechanization Takes Command: A Contribution to Anonymous History*, revd edn (London, 1969), p. 364.

9 John Gloag, *A Social History of Furniture Design* (London, 1966), p. 178.

10 Giedion, *Mechanization Takes Command*, p. 313.

11 Ibid., p. 413.

12 Gloag, A Social History pp. 125–69.

13 Nikolaus Pevsner, 'The Evolution of the Easy Chair', *Architectural Review*, 91 (1942), p. 61.

14 Emile Zola, *Nana*, trans. Burton Rascoe (New York, 1922), p. 28.

15 As quoted in Anne Massey, *Interior Design since 1900*, 3rd edn (London, 2008), p. 124.

16 Tag Gronberg, *Designs on Modernity: Exhibiting the City in 1920s Paris* (Manchester, 1998), p. 42.

17 Lorna Hay, 'Each Room Costs the Same to Furnish, Which Would You Choose To Live In?', *Picture Post* (4 April 1953), p. 18.

18 Galen Cranz, *The Chair: Rethinking Culture, Body and Design* (London, 2000), p. 106.

19 See Sarah Teasley, 'Home-builder or Home-Maker?', *Journal of Design History*, XVIII/1 (2005), pp. 81–97.

20 Ibid., p. 94, note 9.

21 Paul Reilly, 'Postscript (1969)', in David Joel, *Furniture Design Set Free: The British Furniture Revolution, 1851 to the Present Day*, revd edn (London, 1969), p. 101.

22 Stephen King, *On Writing: A Memoir of the Craft* (London, 2000), p. 62.

23 Cranz, *The Chair*, p. 49.

24 James Agee and Walker Evans, *Let Us Now Praise Famous Men* (London, 1969), pp. 137–8.

25 See www.luxurylamb.com (accessed 16 November 2009).

26 See www.nomadwheelchairs.com/blog (accessed 16 November 2009).

27 Ad for BoysStuff.co.uk as featured in *Metro* newspaper, London (26 November 2009).

4 Craft and Materials

1 Thomas H. Ormsbee, *The Windsor Chair* (New York, 1962).

2 *Advices & Queries: The Yearly Meeting of the Religious Society of Friends*

(Quakers) in Britain (London, 1995), p. 15.

3 Marcia Pointon, 'Quakerism and Visual Culture, 1650–1800', *Art History*, XX/3 (1997) p. 399.

4 Edward Tadros, 'The Very Best of British', *Good Housekeeping* (October 2008), p. 233.

5 John Gloag, as quoted in David Joel, *Furniture Design Set Free: The British Furniture Revolution from 1851 to the Present Day* (London, 1969), pp. 15–16.

6 Gustav Stickley, as quoted in Anne Massey, *Interior Design Since 1900* (London, 2008), p. 20.

7 June Sprigg, *Shaker Design* (New York and London, 1986), p. 16.

8 As quoted in Edward Deming Andrews and Faith Andrews, *Religion in Wood: A Book of Shaker Furniture* (Bloomington, IN, 1966), p. xiii.

9 Charles Dickens, 'American Notes', in *The Works of Charles Dickens*, vol. III (New York, 1880), p. 329.

10 *Modern Woman* (July 1925), p. 7, as quoted in Fiona Hackney, 'Use Your Hands for Happiness', *Journal of Design History*, XIX/1 (2006), p. 31.

11 As quoted in Clive Edwards, 'Home is Where the Art is', *Journal of Design History*, XIX/1 (2006), p. 31.

12 *Modern Woman* (28 August 1937), p. 10, as quoted in Hackney, 'Use Your Hands for Happiness', p. 29.

13 Pat Kirkham, 'The Inter-War Handicrafts Revival', in Judy Attfield and Pat Kirkham, *A View From the Interior: Feminism, Women and Design* (London, 1989), p. 180.

14 See http://www.wonderhowto.com/how-to/video/how-to-make-a-homemade-electric-chair (accessed 16 November 2009).

15 As quoted in Edwards, p. 19, C. Beecher and H. B. Stowe, from *The American Woman's Home* 'Home is Where the Art is' (1870).

16 Gareth Williams, *The Furniture Machine: Furniture since 1990* (London, 2006), p. 114.

17 Ibid., p. 11.

18 Peter Christian, 'Hot Seats of Inspiration', *Design Week* (November 1991), p. 11.

19 Peter Christian, 'State of Flux', *Design Week* (16 September 1988), p. 3.

20 Philippe Starck, *The International Design Yearbook*, 1989–90, p. 42.

21 See http://www.heals.co.uk/Soft-Furnishings/Black-Patent-Bean-Bag/invt/788015 &bklist=icat,2,mycatref (accessed 21 April 2009).

22 Rebecca Tanqueray, 'Fashion Shoot', *Sunday Times* (10 June 2007), p. 8.

5 Fine Art Chairs

1 Joanna Woodall, ed., 'Introduction', in *Portraiture: Facing the Subject*, Critical Introductions to Art (Manchester, 1997), p. 2.

2 Alfred Nemeczek, *Van Gogh in Arles* (New York, 1995), p. 10.

3 See www.vam.ac.uk/collections/photography/past_exhns/seeing/chair (accessed 18 November 2009).

4 Richard Hamilton, as quoted in *Richard Hamilton*, exh. cat., Tate Gallery, London (1970), p. 51.

5 As quoted in Jeanne Siegel, *Artwords: Discourse on the 60s and 70s*, 2nd edn (New York, 1992), p. 225.

6 As quoted on www.tate.org.uk/servlet/ViewWork?cgroupid=999999961&workid=7232&searchid=8172&tabview=text (accessed 24 June 2009).

7 Laura Mulvey, 'You Don't Know What's Happening, Do You Mr Jones?', in *Framing Feminism*, ed. Rozsika Parker and Griselda Pollock (London, 1995) p. 128.

8 Lisa Tickner, 'Allen Jones in Retrospect: A Serpentine Review', *Block*, 1 (1979), p. 39.

9 Kelly Dennis, *Art/Porn: A History of Seeing and Touching* (Oxford, 2009), p. 11.

10 Miles Erwin, 'Is This the New Fashion Trend? Yet corset is . . . ', *Metro* (26 November 2009), p. 39.

11 '21st Century Sex', Editorial to *Wallpaper** no. 124 (July 2009).

12 Alice Rawsthorn, 'The Apartment', *Wallpaper**, no. 124 (July 2009), p. 93.

13 Ibid., p. 96.

14 Sally Spinks in e-mail to author (24 June 2009).

15 Margit Emesz, *Take A Seat*, exh. cat., Barbican Art Gallery, London (2008), p. 12.

16 *Telling Tales: Fantasy and Fear in Contemporary Design*, exh. leaflet, Victoria and Albert, Museum, London (2009), p. 1.

17 Ibid., p. 6.

Select Bibliography

Attfield, Judy, *Wild Things: The Material Culture of Everyday Life* (Oxford, 2000)

Auslander, Leora, *Taste and Power: Furnishing Modern France* (London, 1996)

Banham, Reyner, *Modern Chairs, 1918–1970* (London, 1970)

Brilliant, Richard, *Portraiture* (London, 1991)

Brown, Linda, and Deyan Sudjic, *The Modern Chair* (London, 1988)

Crang, Mike, and Nigel Thrift, eds, *Thinking Space* (London, 2000)

Crowley, D. and J. Pavitt, eds, *Cold War Modern: Design, 1945–1970* (London, 2008)

Crowley, John E., *The Invention of Comfort: Sensibilities and Design in Early Modern Britain and Early America* (Baltimore, MD, and London, 2001)

Digital Library for the Decorative Arts and Material Culture, University of Wisconsin-Madison, http://digital.library.wisc.edu/1711.dl/DLDecArts

Emery, Marc, *Furniture by Architects* (New York, 1988)

Fiell, Charlotte, and Peter Fiell, *1000 Chairs* (London, 2005)

Gloag, John, *A Social History of Furniture Design, from BC 1300 to AD 1960* (London, 1966)

Hogben, Carol, *Introduction to Modern Chairs, 1918–1970* (London, 1970)

Jackson, A., and A. Jaffer, eds, *Maharaja: The Splendour of India's Royal Courts* (London, 2009)

Jackson, L. *Robin and Lucienne Day: Pioneers of Contemporary Design* (London, 2001)

Kirkham, Pat, *Charles and Ray Eames: Designers of the Twentieth Century* (Cambridge, MA, and London, 1996)

Ormsbee, Thomas H., *The Windsor Chair* (New York, 1962)

Sparke, Penny, *Furniture* (London, 1986)

Steele, Valerie, *The Corset: A Cultural History* (London, 2001)

Tigerman, Bobby, ' "I Am Not a Decorator": Florence Knoll, the Knoll Planning Unit and the Making of the Modern Office', *Journal of Design History*, XX/1 (Spring 2007), pp. 61–74

Wilk, Christopher, *Marcel Breuer: Furniture and Interiors*, exh. cat., MoMA (New York, 1981)

Williams, Gareth, *The Furniture Machine: Furniture since 1990* (London, 2006)

Woodall, Joanna, ed., *Portraiture: Facing the Subject* (Manchester, 1997)

Acknowledgements

I would like to thank Vivian Constantinopoulos at Reaktion for first suggesting I write this book. My colleagues at Kingston University, London, have been as supportive as ever, and I would like to thank Alice Beard for giving me access to her collection of *Nova* magazine; Peter Christian and Jakki Dehn for sharing the designers' viewpoint; Trevor Keeble for inviting me to give a paper at the 2007 Design History Conference he organized; Harriet McKay for sharing her Union Castle findings; Paul Micklethwaite for opening my eyes to the sustainability agenda; Helen Potkin for giving insight into fine art and the chair; and Penny Sparke for the modern interiors perspective. The Faculty of Art, Design Architecture funded the picture research costs. Students on the 'There's No Place Like Home?' course provided stimulating discussion around the subject. Paul Atkinson and Greg Votolato gave me invaluable peer support and encouragement. Denzil Everett found some great pictures. Special thanks to James Isaac, for helping with photography, good cooking and encouragement to keep me going.

Photo Acknowledgements

The author and the publishers wish to thank the below sources of illustrative material and/or permission to reproduce it.

AllModern.com: p. 125; Courtesy of Ron Arad Associates: p. 165; Author's collection: pp. 93, 112, 116, 187; Courtesy of Derya Aydogdu: p. 208; Courtesy Cat Bagg: p. 205; Collection Alice Beard: p. 124; Thomas Breuer: p. 69; Cassina I Maestri Collection: p. 71; Cassina I Contemporanei Collection/Archivio Gio Ponti: p. 95; Courtesy of the Charleston Trust, photo Tony Treet: p. 157; Culture and Sport Glasgow (Museums): p. 62; Jakki Dehn: p. 173; Courtesy of Droog Design: p. 176; Courtesy of George Eastman House, International Museum of Photography and Film: p. 51; Eco Museum, Saint-Nazaire, Brittany: p. 109; Mary Evans Picture Library: pp. 108, 114; Fritz Hansen: pp. 89, 90, 91; Jim Isaac: pp. 17, 141; Istockphoto: p. 41 (Azndc); Knoll Inc: pp. 67, 79, 80, 82; Ellie Laycock, www.ellielaycock.co.uk: p. 172; Library of Congress, Washington, DC: pp. 8, 140, 152; LoveHoney Ltd: p. 126; Courtesy of John Makepeace Furniture: p. 160; Courtesy of Harriet McKay: p. 11; Memphis Design: pp. 127 (photo © Studio Azzurro), 129 (photo © Roberto Gennari); Herman Miller: pp. 6, 75, 76; © The National Gallery, London: p. 190; National Museum of Wales, Cardiff: p. 193; National Portrait Gallery, London: pp. 183, 185; © Lewis Morley Archive/National Portrait Gallery, London: p. 195; Nomad Design: p. 136; Verner Panton Design: p. 122; Private Collection: p. 151; R20th Century Gallery, New York: p. 161; Race Furniture Ltd: p. 86; Rex Features (Everett Collection): pp. 63, 156; Royal Borough of Kensington and Chelsea (for Linley Sambourne House, 18 Stafford Terrace): p. 37; Photo Scala, Florence: p. 180 (Digital Image, The Museum of Modern Art, New York/ © ARS, NY and DACS, London 2010); Scottish National Gallery of Modern Art, Edinburgh: p. 40; Courtesy of Brooke Shirley: p. 133; Society of Antiquaries, London: p. 58; Courtesy Sally Spinks: p. 204; Starck Network: pp. 168, 169; © Tate, London: pp. 186, 192, 194, 197; Tyne and Wear Museums Service: pp. 44, 45; Courtesy of Studio Patricia Urquiola: p. 178; V&A Images/Victoria & Albert Museum, London: pp. 20, 21, 33, 57, 59, 60, 145, 148, 150; Varier: p. 118; Bruce Wealleans: pp. 14, 42 top left & top right, 52, 54; Wycombe Museum, High Wycombe, Buckinghamshire: pp. 142, 143; Courtesy of Tokujin Yoshioka Inc.: p. 179.

Index